BREAKING
THE
ARGUMENT
CYCLE

How to Stop Fighting **Without** Therapy

SHARON M. RIVKIN, M.A., M.F.T.

life

Guilford, Connecticut

An imprint of Globe Pequot Press

Copyright © 2009 by Sharon M. Rivkin, M.A., M.F.T.

GPP Life is an imprint of Globe Pequot Press.

Text design by Sheryl P. Kober
Layout by Kevin Mak
Cover design by Diana Nuhn

Library of Congress Cataloging-in-Publication Data
Rivkin, Sharon M.
  Breaking the argument cycle : how to stop fighting without therapy / Sharon M. Rivkin.
      p. cm.
  ISBN 978-0-7627-5458-8
 1. Marital conflict. 2. Interpersonal conflict. 3. Problem solving. I. Title.
  HQ734.R593 2009
  646.7'8—dc22
                                        2009024074

Printed in the United States of America

10 9 8 7 6 5 4 3 2 1

To Michael, Talia, and Tashina—
the pearls at the heart of my life.

Transformation

The poison is the remedy. In order to break the argument cycle, we must uncover the root of our conflict, which is also the source of our healing. The clearing we make within ourselves, the freedom we find within our own inner conflict, the ability to turn the poison into a remedy, is the greatest gift we give ourselves.

Contents

Author's Note

Breaking the Argument Cycle is an excellent source that teaches couples how to stop fighting without actually stepping into a therapist's office. However, this does not imply whatsoever that I believe that all issues that result in arguments or drawn-out battles can be resolved without therapy. As a practicing therapist this is neither my message nor my personal philosophy. When and if a couple are in severe distress, a therapist should always be the first course of action. However, because therapy is not an option for every couple in trouble due to various reasons, I felt it necessary to come to their aid by writing this book as an educational tool to help them understand what's going on and present them with options for resolving their repetitive arguments.

Moreover, certain severe and not so severe mental conditions and personality disorders should *always* be treated by a therapist and are beyond the scope of this workbook and the First Argument Technique. Those conditions and disorders do not apply to the core-issue work contained herein.

All of the cases described in this book are composites. Details have been deliberately altered to protect my clients' rights of confidentiality and privacy.

Introduction

One Fourth of July, as I was sitting on a grassy hillside waiting for the fireworks to begin, my mind went straight to a painful groove: my boyfriend, Lucas. For the past two years, we had been in the throes of an intense relationship, and our pattern was one of symbiotic closeness for weeks at a time, alternating with weeks of angry distance. As difficult as our relationship had been from the beginning, we also somehow complemented one another. Lucas always said he was drawn to my warmth. I found him irresistibly handsome with his dark hair, deep brown eyes, and tall and slender build. Even more compelling to me, however, was his decisive, take-charge manner. Because I had grown up in a chaotic household, I often felt like I was on my own and in charge of providing myself with guidance and rules, despite the consistent presence of my mother and father. Part of that I liked, because it taught me independence. But now, as a struggling single mother, I was once again facing a familiar scenario of making everyday and important decisions on my own. Therefore, when Lucas was so sure of himself, with his take-charge attitude and decision-making ease, I felt a sense of awe and relief. Finally someone was taking care of me! The idea that this tall, knowledgeable man was going to help put my life in order seemed too good to be true.

Indeed, it was too good to be true. Lucas had a remarkable way of making fantasy seem real. As if he knew my unspoken desires, he would make promises that I found impossible to resist. He would enumerate the trips that we would take together, describing them in such vivid detail—the cabin by the river, the hot springs in the desert—it was as though they had already happened. He would describe the dream house he was going to build for me, with its bedroom suite, rooms for the kids, and redwood deck. His language was poetic; the simplest things—a window seat or a porch swing—easily ignited a magical visualization of a wondrous life together with him in this elusive dream house. Yet at the same time, he'd take out a pen and piece of paper and make diagrams, complete with estimated measurements, making it all seem real. When the time came for Lucas to fulfill his promises, however, they all simply evaporated. Again and again, I found myself disappointed, let down, and angry in matters both big and small.

As my relationship progressed and my frustrations with Lucas grew, I easily recognized his hot and cold temperaments. When he was feeling generous, he would talk about building a life together. When he wasn't in his big-hearted role, his promises became empty words that were suddenly switched into making me the one who was pressuring him into sketching that dream house or constructing that new deck. And then, when the reality of our dreams was discussed, he acted as if he had never mentioned the plans. Our fights consistently replayed themselves in this same manner. I was constantly questioning my sanity, my hearing, and my perceptions—trying always to appease him, I was persistent in holding back my frustration and anger. These unresolved arguments became so repetitious and so serious that I began to question whether we could really work through these important issues and be together. I didn't really want to break up with him, but then again, I couldn't imagine living like this forever. I was in a continuous state of confusion and despair, feeling stuck in a relationship that I couldn't stay in or get out of. I felt helpless and hopeless to ever change my situation. Nothing I had tried worked, either to make things better or to end the relationship

So it was in the midst of a noisy Fourth of July cel-ebration that all I could hear were the words of our most recent argument pounding in my head. Lucas and I had planned a weekend of planting grass seed in my front yard. On the morning of the project, he arrived at my house in a bad mood. As always, I tried to lighten things up by placating him . . . anything that would create a friendlier attitude toward me. He said we needed a special machine to help with the seeding of the grass, so I dutifully went out to purchase the equipment. By the time I returned, Lucas had already planted the grass seed without me or the machine. I couldn't understand why he had sent me to get a piece of equipment when he clearly didn't need it. When I got angry about having spent money that I really couldn't afford on a machine that he clearly didn't need, all he could say was, "Oops, I didn't realize when I told you to get the machine that I could actually plant the seed without it . . . sorry! I don't know why you always overreact to what I say or ask you to do. What's the big deal about my realizing that I didn't need the machine?"

Lucas's response, though maybe innocent to some-one else, was hurtful to me, because it implied that my feelings didn't count and somehow my memory about the situation was now in question. I knew him well enough at that point to know he was starting a fight with me. Even though he offered to do the work, and all I did was accept that offer, he cleverly turned the situation around and maintained that I was making a big deal out of noth-ing. "What's your problem anyway? I planted your grass just like you wanted me to do."

That response, once again, was the same proverbial knife that dug its way deeper into my heart and soul. For the first time it occurred to me that this fight, though *on the surface* not the same as the others, was nevertheless an extremely familiar scenario of all the arguments we'd had in the past two years. Each argument shared the same old handful of hurtful words and accusations that Lucas would throw at me whenever there was conflict in our relationship. And those wounding words always held an extraordinary power for me all the way back to the beginning of our relationship.

As the Fourth of July festivities continued, I sat alone with only the thoughts of Lucas and an explosive past to keep me company. I continued to replay our most recent fight, tear it apart, and desperately try to make any sense of what actually happened throughout my two years in this relationship. I tried to organize all the pieces of our unhealthy existence as a couple to determine why everything fell apart, but I just couldn't put together this complex puzzle. Something was missing. As my mind started traveling farther back into our relationship and past conflicts, our first argument suddenly hit my awareness as vividly as if it had just occurred.

Lucas and I had agreed that he would build a fence in my backyard. When we began to discuss the details, it was apparent that we had completely different recollections about the original agreement.

SHARON: *So when will you start on the fence?*
LUCAS: *I didn't realize we were at that point. I thought we were still discussing the idea of a fence.*
SHARON: *You're kidding! Don't you remember that we discussed this the other night, and you said you wanted to do it soon, while you had time?*
LUCAS: *What's the big deal? I don't know why you're so upset. All I said was that I didn't realize we had a final agreement. Suit yourself.*

"What's the big deal?" When Lucas asked this question in our very first argument, I felt what I knew to be true was being thrown into question. From that moment on, whenever we had a conflict, the groove from our original argument became deeper, although at the time, I had no idea it was happening. Our fights seemed both trivial, in that the content of the argument was about a fence—or a lawn mower or a stack of wood—and predictable, in that these seemingly innocent topics would cause a major fight between us. I watched the process with each fight, knowing I needed to do something different, and yet it was so difficult to stop the same pattern from repeating itself over and over. He would say the same things to me, and I would say the same things to him. We were getting nowhere quickly. Whatever I was saying was not helping to change me or the situation. I might as well have had a tape recorder to repeat my useless words for all the good they were doing. I was stuck in my own repetitive pattern that was driving me crazy.

Now, as the people around me turned their attention to the noise and lights in the sky, I found myself thinking, "If only I had a glossary to remind me of the words that leave me feeling so powerless and so hooked into this unending pattern!" It was this revelation that prompted me to immediately pull out a pen and scrap of paper from my purse. Then and there, I began to write my glossary:

Suit yourself was my first entry. These words always left me feeling as though I was selfish and all alone in my delusions. My habitual response was to argue in defense of myself. Now I wondered, "How might I answer differently?" I jotted down some alternative responses: "Thank you, I will," or "Okay, I'm glad to take myself into consideration."

What's the big deal? was next. Any intensity on my part would elicit this response from Lucas, making me feel like a hysterical female. Again, how might I respond then and in future fights? Rather than doubting myself and pretending that it wasn't a big deal, I could have said, "It is a big deal, and I'm not going to minimize my feelings or feel badly about feeling this way. I'm angry, and you know why, so stop acting like this is okay, because it isn't." At that point I would have empowered myself, prompting Lucas to respond differently, because we would have broken the familiar pattern that was keeping us stuck. By that response I wouldn't be internalizing his words or allowing him to make me doubt myself. I actually would have said something to him on my own behalf, taking myself into consideration by responding from a new and stronger place, rather than having an automatic reaction to his words.

While writing this second entry, I had a powerful feeling of déjà vu, the sense that this was familiar . . . that I'd been here before. Over the next few weeks this same feeling kept recurring, but I couldn't figure it out or trace it back to its roots. Finally, one night, just as I was on the brink of sleep, I remembered: When I was young, my sister, like many siblings, occasionally called me names, and sometimes she told me I was ugly. She even went so far as to call me *Ug.* Because she was my big sister, and I held her in such esteem and wanted her approval, not to mention how sure of herself she sounded, I believed her. I held the belief that I was ugly for many years without questioning its validity. (This is very common for a child to do with family members. The belief becomes internalized, and we act as if it is true and begin to shape our lives around a false belief.) I carried this belief until one memorable day when I was twelve, I walked into our dining room. In its wall-size mirror, I accidentally caught sight of a very pretty girl with shiny brown hair and bright, dark eyes. To my amazement, that girl was me! I stood there for a long time, gazing with disbelief into a face that was *not* ugly.

Upon having this memory, I realized there was a distinct similarity between my sister and Lucas. Both of them told me things about myself that weren't true! My sister told me I was ugly, and that wasn't true. Lucas told me I forgot certain interactions between us and, therefore, became demanding and ungrateful, even selfish. I knew that wasn't true. Since there was this similarity between my original family dynamics and my present-day relationship dynamics with Lucas, I saw how susceptible I was to his particular form of communication that always left me doubting myself. Because of my earlier experiences, I had a wound of not trusting my own perceptions and beliefs. Although that began to heal when I was twelve after realizing I wasn't ugly, my early beliefs, nevertheless, had many layers. Therefore, in my first argument with Lucas, my old belief that others knew more about me than I knew about myself was triggered again.

Since childhood wounds go deep, they take time to heal. Each relationship we have gives us a new opportunity to repair these deeply wounded layers. Finally I realized that my relationship with Lucas actually had the potential to help me continue to heal that old wound. With that realization, my brain went a step further: I realized that my first argument with Lucas—about the fence—triggered me because it put my beliefs into question. Rather than trust my own memory and knowledge about what happened, my tendency was to believe his truth over my own because I adored him and, like my sister, he seemed so sure of himself. *Could it be that I really had forgotten what he had said about the timing of the fence?* Right away, I was triggered—hooked—into my old childhood pattern of not trusting myself. Because I didn't realize the power of this first argument—that it hooked me back to my original childhood trauma of a little girl who believed she was ugly—I was unable to resolve our first fight. Therefore all of

our subsequent unresolved arguments were simply varia-
tions of the same theme of not trusting my own perceptions. By the time Lucas and I were fighting about seeding
the grass, my pattern of distrusting myself had already
been established with our first argument. What a major
breakthrough that was for me!

After discovering the link between my most recent
argument with Lucas, with our first argument as a couple, and what I have come to call the "story-below-the-
story"—in this case, a little girl called *Ug*—I not only
realized the power of the first argument, I also experienced a remarkable shift in my interactions with Lucas.
From the moment I understood what gave his words
such power over me, those words began to lose their
power. Rather than believe the "truths" told to me by
other people, I was learning to identify and validate my
own truths. Now when he demanded, "What's the big
deal?," I was able to calmly stand my ground, because I
believed myself and my own perceptions rather than his.
Since I was no longer doing my part to fuel our recurrent arguments, they ran out of steam, and the argument
cycle began to break. We had to simply face each other
without the compulsive habit of our conflict. Not only
did I experience a new freedom within our relationship
because we were no longer stuck repeating the same
patterns and arguments over and over again, but I also
felt the possibility of healing a deep childhood wound.

Lucas became very confused when I changed my
behavior and responses to him, and he tried other ways
to get me back into our old pattern. None of his attempts
worked, so our relationship took on a different dynamic. I
held my own ground, which enabled me to see Lucas in a
different light. He didn't have the same kind of power over
me, because I was changing my old childhood pattern of
nonbelief into believing my own truth. When his control

over me began to dissipate, so did our relationship. I knew I needed to end it. As the healing took place within me, I eventually gained enough strength to leave. Although we couldn't heal our actual relationship to enable us to stay together, it nevertheless did heal because we broke the argument cycle that had kept both of us stuck in destructive and dysfunctional patterns. I was also able to heal a deep wound within myself, once I saw that our first argument was connected to my old childhood trauma. This new knowledge helped me choose a better partner for myself in my next relationship and was the catalyst that ended my destructive patterns.

My Three-Step Technique

Gradually I brought what I had discovered from my own personal life into my work as a psychotherapist. Again and again I saw the remarkable power of this simple and amazingly powerful three-step method, what I now refer to as the First Argument Technique, as it miraculously broke the argument cycle and transformed my clients' relationships with the use of three proven steps: *peel, reveal, heal.*

When you shift away from the current conflict to the first argument or major disappointment that you can remember, then *peel* away the topic of that argument, you can immediately locate your personal history, the story-below-the-story that makes you react so strongly. Once you *reveal* the original story of your childhood, a deeper understanding of yourself and your partner emerges, defusing the intense charge around the current conflict. By communicating your story to your partner, anger can turn into understanding and empathy. You can then negotiate a solution with your partner and begin to *heal* the relationship.

This process goes very deep very quickly—yet without needing to dredge up every single childhood memory. Once you discover your story-below-the-story (also known as your core issue), you have simplified the healing process, because you can now go back to that core issue every time you have a fight that *hooks* you into your past. Moreover, these core issues never change throughout the relationship . . . no matter how many years a couple have been together . . . no matter how many kids . . . no matter what the circumstance . . . no matter what the argument. You no longer have to spend hours, days, or a lifetime arguing about the fence or the grass seed, because you now know something deeper: Your story-below-the-story has been triggered, and you're hooked. Since you now know what you're really fighting about, you can drop down to a deeper level of intimate communication with your partner—without fighting, accusing, and blaming—because you're talking about the real issue, not the superficial one that hooked you.

Remember: Not all conflicts turn into heated fights. Issues that don't hook you often get resolved quickly and easily. Therefore, if your response to a situation is disproportionate to the content (you're arguing about a fence as if it was a life or death situation), you know you're hooked into your childhood issues. You wouldn't be fighting if you weren't hooked.

For most couples, revealing the old wounds that lie at the root of their conflict stirs feelings of tenderness for one another and enables them to drop the confusion, hopelessness, and helplessness and gain more clarity about how to proceed in their relationships. *Clarity is healing.* In my relationship with Lucas, after revealing my core issue, we did gain more understanding and empathy for each other, but it was still necessary for me to end the relationship. Clarity enables us to move forward, together or apart, because we know what we're dealing with. Therefore, not only does the First Argument Technique help to build intimacy and clarity, it also reminds each person that he or she has his or her own work to do. For years now I have made use of these discoveries in my psychotherapy practice and in my own personal life, and now I'm making them available to you.

This book contains these unique conflict resolution discoveries and the knowledge and information I have experienced on both a personal and professional level. The first half of the book teaches you about conflict and how it can actually enhance your relationship; how to know when you're hooked and the power of patterns; the process of unhooking and the practice of hope; changing old patterns and the risks involved; affairs as the ultimate relationship challenge; and, finally, the rewards that you can reap after clearing your past. The second half is where the real healing work begins. It starts by entering into my "Therapy Room," a virtual workbook that replicates an actual therapy session you would experience in my own office, as if you were sitting right across from me. Here, through relative case studies and a carefully designed, user-friendly questionnaire, you'll be guided deeply in and through each of the three steps of the First Argument Technique, starting the process with how to uncover your unique and extremely important story-below-the-story. Once you have completed the first two steps of the First Argument Technique—the peel and reveal phases—you'll be directed to the appropriate tools and exercises for change that are necessary to repair and heal your past traumas and current relationship conflicts, and to enlighten you to the proper handling of future arguments, all based on your unique core issue.

Taking the place of costly, professional therapy, within the pages of my Therapy Room, you'll immediately begin to break the argument cycle; transform chaos, confusion, and hopelessness into resolution, clarity, and hope; and make changes within yourself and as a couple. Without leaving your home, this is a hands-on approach that provides effective transformational exercises using all the expert tools that I, as a licensed marriage family therapist, would use to uncover your core issue and help you on the road to healing your relationship. Here is your chance to really see that it is possible to break the argument cycle and heal your relationship, all without stepping into a professional therapy office. This book may be all it takes for you to save your relationship.

• • •

Surrounded by celebrants on that life-changing Fourth of July, I remember looking over my shoulder and asking myself: "Shouldn't I, as a therapist, be beyond such a desperate, makeshift strategy of writing on scraps of paper to figure out why I was so stuck in my current relationship?" Despite my doubts, I continued because I saw no other choice but to work with what I had: a handful of obsessive words and reactive patterns that kept repeating themselves with no resolution. I knew I had to make a change and do something different, or I was going to lose my mind. As I always tell my clients: "We can only start the healing process where we are in the moment and with what we have at that moment." Little did I know that what was unfolding for me that night would turn out to have such a powerful impact on my life and the lives of others. The same words that had kept me stuck had freed me. What began as a last-ditch move to stop the argument cycle, and end the ensuing chaos and confusion of my relationship, because *I just couldn't keep doing the same thing any more!,* has become a method of working and a way of life for me. The power of this experience is not just that I found my way out of a situation that seemed hopeless, but it was that hopelessness that provided the medium of transformation. The recurrent argument led back to its root, the poison became the remedy, and now—through this book that grew out of a scribbled glossary on a single scrap of paper—I share that remedy with you.

CHAPTER 1

Conflict—The Uninvited Guest

Shutting darkness out only intensifies it. When we actively explore the CONFLICT that threatens us, we open the door to resolution and healing.

- Conflict is part of any intimate relationship.
- Use conflict for information; don't shove it underground.
- An argument arises when something important is at stake.
- When you truly discover what is at stake, you do not endanger your relationship; you enhance it by dealing with the conflict.
- Shaming, blaming, and the need to be right are obstacles to constructive arguments.

Conflict, in its most simplistic form, can be viewed as a clash of beliefs between two intimately connected individuals. In its most extreme state, it has the propensity to become all out war. Given this fact, it's no wonder that most people want to avoid conflict at any cost. We somehow think that if we engage in conflict, it will grow out of control and our perfect relationship will be compromised. We would never think to invite conflict into the relationship, because we've never been taught that there is a healing and connective aspect buried in the core of an argument. Conflict, however, when dealt with appropriately, is actually a valuable tool that can bring couples closer rather than pull them apart. In this chapter we will explore how conflict develops and undermines the intimacy in the relationship, how to deal with it, and how it can be productive and valuable.

Cynthia and Allen met when they were both traveling in Rome, and they were instantly attracted to each other. ("He's so tall!" Cynthia thought. "She's so exotic!" thought Allen.) Though now they would probably both admit that the magnetism was mostly physical, at the time they each believed, "At last I have found my soul mate!"

They had a tiny yet perfect wedding a few weeks later in Venice, with a priest who agreed to marry them in a gondola. Allen thought his whole life had fallen into place. He had not only met the woman of his dreams, but before leaving for his vacation in Europe, he'd been offered an important yet fantastic job in California. As Cynthia had given up both her job and her apartment in the Midwest before coming to Italy, he assumed that she'd be returning with him to build a new life in California. But only a few days after the wedding, she told him she would be flying back to spend a month at her parents' house in the Midwest. Though her plans for a family reunion had been in place long before she met Allen, he felt abandoned.

Seven years later, when they came to see me in my office, they were still confronting the same fundamental issue. Allen complained that Cynthia always had to have her way. Cynthia complained that Allen was always trying to impede her, to hold her back. "She's so demanding," he said. "He's always snapping at me," she said.

The Stress of Beginnings

Not all the couples I work with are married or planning to marry, but I'm struck by how many of those who are married tell me that their first serious argument took place very close to their wedding day. Even for those who aren't married, the first argument often occurs in and around a special occasion that—in one way or another, in private or in public—was meant to mark the couple's significance to each other, to declare: "We really are a couple." One gay couple I met told me that they had their first argument when they decided to move in together. They went on a lovely picnic to celebrate and ended up having their first serious argument—over a drop of mustard! Each accused the other of having used the last drop. Five years later, though they are still happily together, they both acknowledge that their core issue (i.e., the real reason they're fighting), continues to be "which one of us is the more selfish one."

Psychiatrists Thomas H. Holmes and Richard H. Rahe developed a list of stressful life events ranked in order of most stressful to least stressful. Getting married was at the top of that list, and not far behind were the death of a spouse and divorce. Of course there are particular reasons why an actual wedding creates so much stress. Even a relatively modest wedding can generate an exhaustive to-do list, requiring that couples pay enormous attention to detail and field an endless stream of decisions, in addition to juggling financial anxiety and the varying expectations of two families. For many couples, planning a wedding creates unprecedented tension in their power dynamic and places enormous pressure on their capacity to give and take, initiate, and accommodate.

Below these more obvious stressors deeper pressures bear on the wedding couple. Many people don't know how they really feel about a decision until after they've made it or after they've shared the news with others. Whenever that precise moment may be, it's as though the exit door closes and the reality of commitment weighs down as never before. Suddenly the stakes are so high that even a question like, "Are we going to use paper napkins at the reception?" easily becomes the question, "What kind of a life are we going to create together?"

A wedding is meant to be the perfect day, and each partner tends to invest it with his or her vision of the ideal life. Is it any wonder, then, that a clash of ideals often results? And when the clash occurs, is it surprising that the bitterness can be so acute? When planning a wedding and looking forward to a new life together, it is important for a couple to remember that they are two different people from two different families, and a clash in opinions and desires is almost guaranteed to happen. But if each can learn, at the beginning of the relationship, that conflict can actually become a means to better communication, as well as a tool to teach them more about each other and what's important to them, then conflict doesn't have to be threatening or scary.

Finding Your Core Issues

Months before Hilary and Kyle got married, Kyle told Hilary that he wanted to dance with her at their wedding. Hilary agreed, and Kyle signed up for dancing lessons; sometimes they went together, and sometimes Kyle went by himself. At home he practiced diligently. But when the day arrived, they discovered that the train on Hilary's dress made it too awkward for them to dance together. Kyle was terribly disappointed. To make matters worse, Kyle had clearly told Hilary that he didn't want her to stuff cake in his mouth, but she went ahead and did it anyway. When his face burned red with embarrassment, as he'd told her it would, she laughed at him. "Don't take it so seriously!" she said. "It's just a little frosting on your face. Everybody does it."

To Kyle, of course, it wasn't "just a little frosting." And not being able to dance wasn't just a little glitch, either. When Kyle was a child, his older siblings mercilessly teased him. Though he's a very attractive man, he has little natural self-confidence, and it matters a great deal to him that he appears handsome, graceful, poised, and self-assured. Having trampled on Hilary's satin train as he tried to dance with her and then having cake smashed on his face, he felt humiliated by her and doubly betrayed.

Around the time of their first anniversary, Kyle and Hilary came to my office and by then were in crisis. They were constantly arguing, and Kyle had reached the point of telling Hilary that he didn't love her anymore. Kyle said that Hilary never took his feelings into account, and Hilary said that Kyle was impossibly critical. She felt she could do nothing right. Most of their arguments were about the house. "She doesn't understand that I like things to look good," Kyle said. Hilary complained, "If there's a pillow out of place, he has a fit."

Though they had barely been married a year, theirs was among the most hostile relationships I have ever witnessed. Kyle seemed to feel that Hilary was on a secret mission to thwart him, while Hilary felt that Kyle tormented her by seizing on her every flaw and magnifying it out of proportion. When they stepped into my office that first time, I felt the air grow heavy with tension. Although I've worked in this field for many years, I still have moments when my heart sinks and I have to keep myself from bolting out the door. What if this time we just couldn't find the slightest opening in the wall of anger and frustration?

They went on for a while, each piling up the "evidence" against the other as if laying wood for a huge bonfire of insult and injury. Then I took a deep breath and asked them, "Do you remember your first argument?"

With only the slightest pause, as if the memory was just below the surface, Kyle began to describe his bitter disappointment on their wedding day. As he did, Hilary listened with amazement. "I had no idea you were still so upset about that," she said. In fact they both seemed a bit stunned. It hadn't occurred to them that this incident remained unresolved. Yet now that it was out on the table, they could see they were still struggling with the same conflict, the same dynamic.

As with so many other couples I have counseled, this realization did not bring a sense of hopeless entrapment—it brought relief, for they both knew that on their wedding day, neither had been plotting to thwart or torment the other. In going back to their first argument with the use of the First Argument Technique (discussed on page 17), they were able to recover a sense of the basic innocence of their core conflict, which was the real source of tension between them. They could see that the deep anger built up toward one another stemmed from their unresolved first argument, which had kept them constantly stuck in the argument cycle. Hilary and Kyle's relationship exemplified how something that starts out so innocent—a first disagreement, a first hurt—within a year can became almost a "war." Without getting to the real root of the argument, or the core issues, their fights escalated because they were simply arguing about the wrong things. If they had known that they really weren't arguing about pillows on a couch, they could have talked about the true issues and avoided a year of fighting. Once they began to understand that the tension between them had roots that went much deeper than any conscious intention, and rather than dig themselves deeper into the same hard soil of resentment and blame, their task now was to understand those roots.

Though it had been only a year since their first conflict

revealed itself, it had been a long and painful year for both of them—a year that had brought them to the brink of separation. Just think what unhappiness might have been avoided if they had been able to get to the root of that conflict when it first arose—if not on the wedding day itself, then in the days that followed. Sadly, as strong as the tendency is for a couple to have their first argument close to the time of their wedding, there's an equally strong tendency to avoid facing this argument. The very idealism that contributes to the stress of a wedding and increases the likelihood of conflict also reinforces the tendency to bury the conflict, to discount it or deny it.

The Power of Fantasy

In this day and age, there's an addictive quality to our collective fantasy life. It's ironic that so many beliefs and traditions from the past have been shed as "quaint" or "superstitious," yet when it comes to love, we still cling to a fairy-tale version of "happily ever after." Even when, time after time, we experience the crash of disillusionment, we go back to the fantasy for the temporary high of romance, the intoxicating feeling of being in love, that feeling that seems to make everything right in our world.

Most of us grew up hearing fairy tales, and we want those same happily-ever-after endings to happen to us. Even if rationally we know that fairy tales are based on fantasy, it is still very compelling to fantasize in our own relationships, telling ourselves a story that everything is really going to be okay and whatever is happening is not as bad as it might look or feel. Through fantasy, people make excuses for their relationship problems. For instance, in a fairy tale, "The Princess is rescued by the Prince." In reality, however, it's more like, "My Prince just stood me up again!" or "My Princess doesn't even want to dance with me at our own wedding!"

If you remain in reality, you might have to admit that something is wrong in the relationship. And if something is wrong, you may have to confront your partner, which is sure to be uncomfortable and anxiety producing. So you would rather go back into the fantasy where whatever problems you have can be forgotten and, hopefully, nothing bad will ever come of them. Therefore, our fantasy of the relationship helps us to put off dealing with the reality of the situation. As Scarlett O'Hara said in *Gone with the Wind*, "I'll worry about that tomorrow."

Do we cling so tenaciously because deep down we really do recognize the shadow side of the fairy tale, that other side of the story where relationships are hard work and the honeymoon phase lasts only a short time? Do we cling to the fantasy as long as we can because in our hearts we know how many marriages end in the pain of divorce? Because in a world that often feels difficult, scary, and dark, we want something in our lives that is light and almost unreal? Who wants to face reality and its hardships anyway? Isn't the beginning of a relationship the time, of all times, to accentuate the positive? Shouldn't we be more understanding of our partner and not cause a fight? We should be able to deal with this! Whatever the reasons, we have a powerful drive to close our eyes to the first sign of conflict. Yet so many times I've heard people reflect, "If only . . ."

Devin fell in love with Maryann's beauty and wondered why someone as lovely as she would want him. Their first conflict arose when she became suddenly angry at him for what she perceived to be criticism from him. She threatened to end the relationship. Immediately he tried to ignore his angry reaction by saying she was just in a bad mood, and this was probably nothing to worry about. Therefore, he swept his reaction under the rug. However, her sudden, extreme behavior continued for many years, and he was repeatedly hurt and angered by it. He never knew what to do to change their interactions; therefore he ignored his feelings most of the time, because he didn't want to lose her. Instead of focusing on the reality of their failing relationship, Devin held on to the fantasy of Maryann . . . the fantasy of what life was *supposed* to be like with her and what he *hoped* and *wished* for it to be. Because he didn't want to give up his fantasy of the perfect woman and the perfect relationship, he wouldn't face the reality that his marriage was falling apart. He clung tenaciously to his fantasy, until one shocking and devastating day Devin's fantasy collided with reality. Maryann left him. He never saw it coming, because he had convinced himself that his fantasies were real.

Most people don't like to deal with reality if it doesn't match their fantasy. We become habituated to the high of the fantastical moments and tell ourselves that the fantasy is the real relationship—not that other one that is so painful. We are conflicted within ourselves because the reality is not good, so we long to return to the fantasy. I experienced this with Lucas upon seeing a house in Arizona that made me think of the fantasy house he had promised me. Sadly knowing, however, that my fantasy would never come true led me to realize, in that instant that I was in love with the *fantasy* of Lucas, not the Lucas of *reality.* My fantasy was so powerful that I was really grieving the end of my dream more than the end of Lucas being in my life.

We hold on to our fantasy relationship, like Devin did and like I did, hoping it will become a reality. This actually only brings us more pain than if we had let the conflict in and dealt with it from the beginning. What we don't realize is that holding on to the fantasy leaves us unprepared to deal with the reality of our situation and the ability to make changes.

Brett and Sondra were another bride and groom for whom to dance or not to dance had been the first point of serious disagreement. A wedding is already highly symbolically charged, and dancing carries its own weight of meaning. After all, as couples move—or do not move—across the dance floor, they are implicitly asking such questions as: *Are we in step with each other? Who follows, who leads? Do we find pleasure in similar activities? Are we able to make compromises for one another?*

Brett very much wanted to dance at their wedding, but Sondra refused, insisting that she was a hopelessly clumsy dancer and didn't want to embarrass either of them. "You go ahead, I'll watch," she told him, apparently without any rancor. Nevertheless, Brett felt terribly let down. On their first visit to my office, he told me that this had become their pattern: "It's always the same thing. I propose we do something together, and she refuses. She's perfectly pleasant about it, but the fact is, she always says no to new experiences."

Now, looking back over ten years of frustration, Brett wished he had let Sondra know from the very beginning how much that first no to dancing together had hurt him. Not wanting to darken the cloud any further on their wedding day, he hadn't said anything at the time, but the cloud had never gone away. Indeed as their presence in my office showed, with time it had only grown heavier and more oppressive. As painful as it was for Sondra to realize the ramifications of their first disagreement, she too could not help but wish that Brett had let her in on the great storehouse of longing and disappointment he'd been hoarding.

Most couples have the same reaction when they finally realize the repetitive nature of their basic conflict. They fervently wish they'd had the courage to fully open to the conflict when it first arose; precisely then, in the beginning, when things were fresh between them and there was such an abundance of hope. It comforts them a little, just a little, when I tell them, "Well, that's why you didn't face it then; you didn't want to spoil the freshness, to dampen the hope."

The trouble is, of course, that the impulse to preserve the pristine state of the relationship is futile. For whether it comes early or late in a relationship, conflict inevitably arises. And once it does, it doesn't just disappear. It's like the "thirteenth fairy"—the one that Sleeping Beauty's parents didn't invite to the baby's christening because she was equated with negativity . . . precisely the one we don't want to invite to our wedding or into our relationship. In trying to keep her dark energy out of Sleeping Beauty's celebration, her dark energy simply intensified because she was angry about being left out, so she ultimately put a curse on the Princess. That is how conflict works if we ignore it—it comes back with a vengeance. If we can make a place for conflict when it first arrives—not shoo it out the door, shove it under the rug, or bury it in the vault of the heart —we can actually enhance the future of our relationship, not endanger it as we so fear. Once a couple identify their thirteenth fairy, or their core conflict (the true reason they're fighting), I encourage them to retroactively invite this conflict to the celebration, to participate, to be a part of the relationship. Remember: This early conflict, when invited in, has the potential to heal.

The Nature of Argument

An argument can be seen as a kind of dance—not a smoothly flowing waltz to be sure, but a fiery, energetic interaction between two people. Perhaps most like a tango, in which two separate and equally dynamic partners come together and move apart, an argument is a stage upon which couples engage with intensity, each person challenging the other to make original moves within the pattern of the relationship.

Perhaps some people cannot immediately relate to the dance metaphor. "Sounds great!" they might say. "But when I argue with my partner, it feels a lot more like a train wreck than a tango!" What if, rather than dismissing the metaphor out of hand, we were to ask, "What keeps an argument from being more dance-like?" Let's explore that question.

To begin, let's ask the question, what is an argument? For our purposes, an argument is a clash of beliefs, desires, and/or expectations between two intimately connected individuals. If two people are truly alive to themselves and to each other, arguments inevitably arise between them. As we will explore in more detail in the next chapter, it is actually rather worrisome when a couple insist that they never argue. Usually this means at least one of three things: (1) The partners are highly fused and enmeshed with one another and can't bear any degree of differentiation. This causes both partners to be in constant fear of abandonment, feeling they can't live without the other person. This can perpetuate controlling and jealous behaviors when their partner is away from them or has any kind of separate identity; (2) one of the partners has completely surrendered to the will of the other (which would appear in emotionally and/or physically abusive couples); or (3) one or both are extremely passive or indifferent about their shared circumstances. In rare cases, though, it means that the partners are so adept at understanding themselves and each other that they are able to nip conflict in the bud.

A relationship that is completely devoid of conflict

tends to be a relationship without vitality. Though conflict is uncomfortable, and we often don't know how to deal with it, it does have its own energy and can be a compelling force that when dealt with correctly—as we will discuss later with the First Argument Technique—can be an opportunity for growth and change within the relationship. When a couple are lacking vitality and energy between them, they often feel stuck and in a rut with each other.

Arguments arise because something important is at stake—there is an issue that we care about, and there is a person whose response matters to us. When we learn to truly make use of and move through our arguments, they can lead us to a level of intimacy that is deep and vitally dynamic. Rather than move right into our defensive behavior, we can learn to stay open, receptive, and curious. This receptivity permits a true exchange with our partner, an energetic exchange of information that, in its fluid and mutual responsiveness, is dance-like. The goal, then, is not to eliminate arguments altogether, but to find release from those essentially static arguments that, for all their sound and fury, simply slam us again and again against the same wall.

The Three Great Obstacles

What makes for these fruitless arguments? As the Israeli poet Yehuda Amichai wrote,

> From the place where we are right
> flowers will never grow
> in the spring.

Most of us have not been taught how to fight fairly or constructively. When we're angry, we tend to go with our instincts by yelling, blaming, and shaming, trying desperately to get our partner to hear us. Sometimes our natural instincts do not serve us, because they can create destructive fighting patterns that impose pain and hurt on our partner. There are three great obstacles to constructive fighting, which will be discussed in this chapter. By learning what *not to do,* you can learn what you *can do* to resolve an argument without damaging yourself or your partner. You'll see that it is actually possible to gain satisfaction from a fight because both partners are heard and old behaviors are changed.

Obstacle 1: The Need To Be Right

Perhaps more than anything, what solidifies conflict is a rigid and ultimately destructive stance—the need to be absolutely right. As much as we live in a romantic culture, one that constantly reinforces the myth of a blissful, conflict-free "true love," we also live in a very argumentative culture. This is a difficult combination. In our romantic idealism we tend to ignore the first sign of conflict at the precise time it could be most simply addressed. Yet once that conflict breaks out into the open, we tend to frame it in polarizing terms, arguing about who is right or who is wrong, rather than dealing with the real underlying issues.

Turn on the television or radio at virtually any time of day, and you're likely to hear some controversial issue being discussed in terms of conflicting, incompatible points of view. Generally the person who can give the most watertight argument for the absolute rightness of his or her position is the one we declare the winner. And often, in our litigious culture where lawsuits are sometimes filed for the most ludicrous reasons, the "winner" of the conflict not only prevails in the fight, but can walk away with hundreds of thousands of dollars.

In interpersonal relationships, however, "winning"

tends to come at a high cost. For although one person may concede to the verbal power of the other, such power is rarely truly convincing. If one simply feels demoralized and crushed by the other's verbal dexterity, the recipient of the verbal blows is unlikely to experience a real change of heart. The humiliation that results merely adds fuel to the fire of each person involved, and it will erupt with even greater intensity the next time around.

Furthermore, the seeming rationality of one's rightness can mask the emotional reality of the conflict. Rather than talk about feelings of vulnerability, abandonment, fear, or anxiety, it seems easier in the short run just to make a good case for being right. This helps to account for the amazingly fine points one comes up with in an argument and on which people can get stuck. However, these fine points or minute definitions and descriptions of the situation, designed only to prove one's point, are not the true reason for the fight. For example, Judy's ongoing issue with her second husband, Chuck, was that he failed to properly encourage her young son (his stepson). "What about the other day when he was playing baseball?" she asked. "He made a hit, and you didn't even compliment him on it!" "Don't say he made a hit!" her husband insisted. "He hit the ball, but the outfielder caught it, and he didn't get any bases. So that's not a hit!" Chuck's comeback was on the precise definition (*a fine point*) of a hit, but it did not reflect what the argument was truly about It wasn't until the end of our session (with the use of the First Argument Technique discussed on page 17) that Chuck could admit that he wanted his wife's love for himself alone, which stemmed from the fact that his mother ignored him and he never felt special to her. Therefore, when his wife made her son a priority in her life, Chuck was extremely envious of his stepson. He wished he had gotten that kind of attention from his mother. As we can see from this example, there is a certain comfort in being *right* in the face of intense emotion, thus masking what is truly at stake—a deep feeling that is extremely uncomfortable to divulge. It was easier for Chuck to get caught in the seemingly rational, nitpicking argument over the definition of a hit rather than reveal his emotional vulnerability. This example shows us how "being right" covered the reality that underneath the need to be right was a hurt little boy (Chuck) who was still looking for someone to love him unconditionally.

If we continually mask our deepest feelings with the need to be right, we drive a wedge deeper and deeper into the very foundation of our relationship. When we cast blame onto our partner and never get to the root of the conflict, we end up hurting our partner a little bit more each time we fight. In our effort to get our point across, we use hurtful examples of why we're right. We hit below the belt, bringing up past unresolved issues, calling our partner names, or accusing him or her of everything and anything we can think of that bothers us.

The early arguments don't hurt as much as subsequent ones, because there's not a mound of unresolved material. Each time we get hurt in an argument and feel our partner doesn't hear us or see our point, our pain cuts deeper. What we really want deep down is to be heard and seen. However, that gets lost in our resentment and frustrations so that all we want is for our partner to hurt as much as we do. Therefore, the wall between two people builds up so high with pain and suffering that they begin to lose feelings for each other and become numb. Unless the proper tools are used to start tearing down the wall, the division can eventually bring destruction to the relationship. The three-step First Argument Technique is an effective tool that helps tear down that wall of pain and resentment, revealing each partner's core issue, thereby facilitating clarity, which leads to change and healing. Before discussing Obstacle 2, the following brief example shows how to use this three-step process.

Applying the First Argument Technique
The First Argument Technique uses the *peel, reveal, heal* method of problem solving as a way to understand the root dynamics of a relationship. This is the same technique I used with Chuck and his wife Judy to discuss his anger over when is a hit really a hit. I first asked Chuck and Judy if they remembered their first argument. They did, and it was over a similar issue. Judy had taken her son's homework to him at school after he forgot it in the morning. Chuck was furious and said that wasn't right and that her son should just suffer the consequences of forgetting his homework. After all, that's what would have happened to Chuck when he was a young boy. Their first argument was about who was right, just as their current conflict was about who had the right definition of a hit. At Chuck's point, having established that they were having basically the same conflict as they had had at the beginning of their relationship (who's right about issues involving Judy's son), I asked him my next question: *Do you think your fury around the hit issue was an extreme reaction to a simple occurrence?* He agreed that it was. I told him that meant he was being triggered by something in his past or he wouldn't have felt so angry. Once he knew this was a possibility, Chuck could begin to *peel* away the angry reaction and ask himself if he'd ever had these feelings before. When he remembered back, he *revealed* that his mother ignored him and he felt abandoned and unloved for most of his childhood. Once Chuck realized this, by using the first two steps of *peel* and *reveal,* he was able to tell Judy that he was envious of her son because she paid attention to him. He got angry, not really about the homework or the hit, but because

he never received that kind of love and caring from his mother. When Judy gave that love to her son, Chuck's old feelings of neglect and being worthless surfaced. Once his old feelings surfaced and he felt uncomfortable, he began to cover up these more vulnerable feelings by trying to prove that he was right. At the time, he had no idea why he felt so compelled to prove his point.

After Chuck discovered the reason for his strong reaction, through the use of the First Argument Technique, he was able to talk about his feelings of envy and realize that those feelings came from a "hurt little boy" who still was looking for love from his mother. Again, with the use of the three-step First Argument Technique of peel, reveal, and heal, Chuck was able to *peel* back (step one) the content issue of the argument (was it a hit?) and *reveal* (step two) to himself and his wife the feelings of the "hurt little boy." At this point, Judy no longer felt she was being attacked and was able to see and understand Chuck's struggle. Now she felt compassion rather than anger for him; she understood that he masked his core issue of being a "hurt little boy" by arguing with her. Chuck realized that he didn't want to feel resentful about Judy and her son, yet his angry behavior and *need to be right* were triggered by past feelings. Once he understood the root of his conflict, Chuck was able to begin to change his reaction to Judy and his stepson, and *healing* took place.

When you argue about who's right and who's wrong, it's a sign that you're dealing with the surface issues of the argument—the fence, the wastebasket, the hit. You are trying to build a case against each other, hoping that if you can prove your point, your partner will immediately back down from his or her right position and thus suddenly understand what you're saying, agree with you, show you the love and respect you desperately want . . . and then *everything will be all right!* We equate being right with being okay, because we feel validated when we're right. It's a way we can self-evaluate and give ourselves a pat on the back, because we seemingly know more about something than our partner does—and doesn't that just make us the greatest?! If we're right, it's proof in our own minds that we have value. That's why many couples "fight to the death" just to be right, because, conversely, if they're wrong, they don't have as much value in their own minds. We all want to feel good about ourselves, but needing to be right is only a quick and temporary fix to make that happen.

What we learn when we use the First Argument Technique is that when we go beyond the surface of our fights, we switch from needing to be right to needing to understand what makes us react in certain ways and being able to communicate this to our partner. That is why we often don't get the relief and joy that we thought we'd get by winning an argument. It mystifies us that sometimes the win feels empty. This is because it's really the resolution and moving ahead that makes us feel satisfied . . . not being "right."

Given this information, the First Argument Technique becomes relevant and crucial to every couple. It leads us to the root of the argument, which dates back to our childhood issues—the story-below-the-story (also referred to as the "core issue" and discussed in detail in Chapter 2)—which is the true reason why the fight occurred in the first place. The first argument we ever have with our partner or anyone that matters to us taps into our story-below-the-story and triggers an old reaction. Until we understand this, we will have the same argument in different forms throughout our entire relationship.

My clients, more often than not, tell me, "We're still having the same fight as we did from the very beginning of our relationship, and it has never gotten resolved. We have no idea how to change this." As in Chuck's case, the core issue was not about the definition of a hit, it was about his feelings surrounding his mother, who didn't treat him as well as Chuck's wife was treating her son. The First Argument Technique has the ability to take the argument *out of your head* (who's right or who's wrong) and *into your feelings,* which is the real reason you're mad, angry, or hurt. To be able to let go of proving your point or fighting about who's right or wrong, is to begin the healing process. Looking at your story-below-the-story takes you from a divisive method of communicating to one of inclusion and compassion. It's better to ask, "Why am I so upset, and when did I first start to feel this way? What's really bothering me? I don't think this can really be about whether my wife and I agree on the definition of a hit in baseball. That seems too trivial for the amount of anger I'm feeling now." By letting go of who's right and who's wrong, and taking the argument to a deeper level, you'll be able to resolve the argument, because the real reason you're fighting will be revealed. No long-lasting resolution ever comes from a right-or-wrong argument.

What about the wife who is *right* that her husband shouldn't have spent $40,000 on a new car for himself without consulting her? Or the husband who's right that his wife shouldn't have gone off for three days without letting him know where she was? Certainly their protestations are valid and a world away from nitpicking. I don't mean in the least to imply that there is never any right or wrong in what happens between a couple. But I've worked in the field of couples therapy for over twenty eight years, and I know it's vital to acknowledge that if a couple are going to resolve their repetitive conflict, no matter how grave the issue at stake, the time inevitably comes when "I'm right, you're wrong" needs to be put aside if there's any chance of a resolution to the constant battles. Even if you feel you're right beyond a shadow of a doubt, and maybe you are, you have to think about the bottom line: Is being right helping you to resolve your conflict? Is it bringing peace and love into your relationship? If not, that is precisely the reason why you need to find a new way to communicate so that your arguments can finally be resolved, with lasting intimacy created in your relationship.

In the following chapters and workbook, you'll fully explore how using the First Argument Technique of peeling the surface issue to reveal the story-below-the-story can release you from the polarizing grip of right and wrong. Next, we'll explore the two other obstacles that create relationship deadlock.

Obstacle 2: Blaming

Blaming, which tends to go along with being right, is another pattern that immobilizes couples. Blaming, by its very nature, stays focused on the surface issue of the conflict, like fighting about a fence, grass seed, or a baseball hit. "You started it." "It happened because of what you did." Phrases such as these become the focal point of the argument, and blaming the other person for the predicament that both partners are in is very common. We rarely start off by taking responsibility for our part in a fight. It's usually easier to see fault in another person rather than in ourselves. We blame because we think that if we can show our partner that they are worse than we are—more at fault than we are—then they'll stop blaming us. Unfortunately, all we do is continue the argument, alternating between attacking and defending. "I'm not as bad as you, and I'm going to prove it." "No you're not, because I'm going to prove it first!" And so it goes, when we feel attacked, we defend, but we never resolve the conflict.

Blaming comes from being fixated on unresolved arguments of the past, so it's hard to move toward a new solution. When a couple have been in conflict for some time, it's often because each partner is holding a long chain of blame. ("You wouldn't go with me to my office party last week. You didn't want to go skiing three weeks ago. And before that, you canceled that cruise we were going to take. And before that . . ..") When couples are able to grasp the power of their first argument to see that the long chain of blame goes back to a first incident ("You wouldn't dance with me at our wedding!"), suddenly an ocean of resentment can be distilled into a single—potent—drop. And, as we will see, that distilled form makes it much more possible for a couple to get to the root of their repeated conflict through the lens of compassionate curiosity. ("You know, after all these years, I've never really understood why it was so important to you that we dance at our wedding. Why don't you try to tell me?")

The quickest and best way to stop blaming your partner is to take responsibility for your part in the argument. Stop saying *you* and start saying *I*. When you do this, you invite your partner to do the same. When you blame your partner, you do not make it a safe environment to share feelings. No one is going to share deep feelings if they feel they are being attacked. Once you talk about yourself and your struggle, your partner will have more compassion for you and be more willing to share in return.

Breaking old habits can feel overwhelming, so remember that just because you've learned that blaming isn't a good or efficient way to resolve arguments doesn't mean that you'll never fall into blaming again. What it does mean is that if you find yourself blaming your partner, you will be less likely to *continue* to blame because a seed has been planted that it doesn't work. Whenever either of you realizes the futility of blaming, you have new tools to change the argument immediately into a dialogue.

Maya and Timothy were arguing about whose turn it was to feed the dog. Maya said, "I always feed the dog, and he's yours, too. How come you never remember it's your turn to feed him?" Timothy countered with, "What do you mean? I just fed him yesterday! Did you conveniently forget that already?" Maya suddenly realized they were back in their old bad habit of blaming and, though she still thought she had fed the dog the night before, she changed her approach and said, "Hey, Timothy, here we are blaming each other again, and we both know that doesn't work, so let me rephrase my last comment. What I meant to say was, I'm really busy right now and I'd appreciate it if you would feed Jasper (the dog) tonight. It really doesn't matter who's turn it is. I know we both love him and take care of him equally." When put that way, with Timothy not feeling blamed, he responded, "You're right, and of course I'll feed Jasper. Thanks for getting us back on track with our communication." Maya did not feel weak or defeated when she stopped blaming Timothy about the dog. She actually felt strong and good about herself, because she was able to take responsibility for her part of the fight and change its direction. In the midst of blaming Timothy, she remembered that her goal was resolution, not blaming.

Obstacle 3: Shaming
Shaming, or expressing contempt for another's very being, is also high on the list of obstacles. When shame is brought into an argument, we move from focusing on an issue to attacking the person—from, "You didn't dance with me at our wedding," to "You can't bear to see me happy." How could anyone respond, except very defensively, to such a declaration? Shaming is particularly

damaging for two reasons. First, it tends to globalize or exaggerate the conflict to such a degree that it's impossible to know exactly where to begin in responding to the accusing partner and how to respond to the accusations. When we feel shamed, we usually close down and protect ourselves.

Second, if we communicate to someone that we are disgusted, not by a particular behavior, but by who he or she is, then we attack the very ground of intimacy that we have built with that person. There's a big difference between saying, "You're a selfish person who never thinks of anyone but yourself. I hate you!" to saying, "What you just said to me is not okay. I don't like how you're treating me. It makes me feel badly about myself." Character assassination and shaming erode trust and intimacy because they literally attack a person at his or her very core. It sends the message, "Not only do you make me mad, but there's something wrong with you. You are sick, mean, and awful."

After many years of fighting and saying shaming things to each other, the love a couple once had begins to disappear and is replaced with hostility and hate. When a partner attacks the foundation of the relationship, he or she runs the risk of destroying any love and goodwill, which makes salvaging the relationship especially difficult. This extreme form of shaming leads to contempt. In fact, it has been found that one of the best predictors of divorce is a marked tendency, of at least one partner, to express contempt. The essence of contempt is a withering gaze that dries up the possibility of growth and change. Why should we want to change for someone who seems to have given up on both the relationship and us?

To deal with contempt for your partner, remember: No matter how angry you might be, you did once love this person, and neither of you started off the relationship trying to hurt each other. Therefore, if you find that contempt has entered into your relationship, go back in time and remember why you fell in love in the first place, giving the good feelings for each other a chance to resurface, which will allow the shaming and contempt to begin to dissipate. In addition, remember that the hurt has come from years of unresolved arguments that have become nastier as each person tries to explain his or her feelings without being heard. Once you have identified your first argument, it's never too late to go back and start to resolve it. This is a powerful tool to use to dissipate the contempt that has built up.

The need to be absolutely right, to blame, and to shame are three major obstacles to constructive arguments. But they are not the only ones. Cultural differences can make it difficult for a couple to interpret one another's responses. Gender differences, too, can play an important role in perpetuating conflict (these are beyond the scope of this book, and a wealth of readily available information about them exists). Not surprisingly, these differences tend to already be present in the first argument, and learning to discern them in that first seed of conflict can go a long way toward making them less overwhelming.

Time and Frame

For now, let's deal with a relatively simple, yet tricky, factor: timing. Knowing when to raise a sensitive issue with your partner or when to let it drop is part of the art of constructive arguing. *Timing is everything.* In general it's better not to raise an issue during the heated moment in which it arises, but to wait until the acute tension dissipates. When you approach a subject at the wrong time, even if you have a good point, your partner will not hear its significance and importance. Conversely, if the timing is right, even the most difficult topics can be broached and discussed successfully.

How do you know when the right time is? First, it's never in the heat of the moment, because your anger will outweigh and impinge on your thinking and communication skills. You will speak regrettable words in an extreme way, which will deeply hurt your partner. Words pack a powerful punch, and the sting and damage will not be remedied by an "I'm sorry."

In the heat of the moment, if you find you're so angry that you can't see straight, take time to cool down and arrange another, less-heated time to talk with your partner about your feelings.

Second, it's difficult to resolve issues when either or both of you are tired or stressed. Don't sweep the argument under the rug, but agree on a different time to discuss the issues.

Third, don't try to resolve issues when you're both busy or running out the door. At these times you risk rushing your discussions and blurting out accusations that will unnecessarily hurt your partner, because anxiety has taken over. Learn to tolerate some anxiety for the sake of good timing. When anxious, take a deep breath, count to ten, call a friend, or write in your journal. Many a truth, even a difficult one, can be spoken in a compassionate way at the *right time,* helping to resolve the argument rather than escalate it.

So, when *is* the right time to resolve a conflict? Ideally, if the interval is not too long, wait for a moment when you and your partner are feeling particularly close and harmonious. This can be quite hard to do, especially for a couple experiencing a great deal of conflict. When a happy moment finally arrives, who wants to spoil it by bringing up a problem? There's that thirteenth fairy again, the one we want to keep out of the celebration, the one that represents conflict. Therefore, the best time to address conflict in an ongoing relationship is when there is maximum trust in the atmosphere. Of course, if the happy moments are infrequent or nonexistent, then it's best not to wait more than a few days before bringing up a touchy subject. Try to set aside a specific date and time to have your discussion. This will allow each person to prepare for the talk and avoid either person feeling surprised by a confrontation.

When you're deciding on the best date and time to talk, it is important to have the right frame for this, or the best possible scenario for addressing difficult issues. To determine this, take the following into consideration:

1. Have you had enough of a time-out to feel less heated within yourselves?

2. Do you have enough time and energy to spend together to work toward a resolution and understanding of the fight?

3. Do you have a good place to have the discussion, such as a private place with no phone calls, children, or other distractions?

If you don't have a specific date and time to talk about your issues, yet feel you've picked the best moment to take the plunge, the next thing to consider is how to broach the subject. A good opening line simultaneously warns your partner that you're about to raise a difficult issue and reassures him or her that you're not going on the attack. For example, imagine a couple in their car, returning from an enjoyable dinner party at their friends' home. One partner might say, "I know we've had a really great evening and neither of us wants to spoil it; however, there is something that's still bothering me from the other day. I'd like to try and talk about it with you now, while we're both feeling relaxed." If the other partner is emphatic that now is not a good time, then it's perfectly reasonable to say, "Okay, but this is really important to me, so I'd like to know when would be a good time." This is an important move to make, actually, because it enlists the other partner's cooperation in setting up a time. It is, in itself, a first step to negotiating.

When you've picked your discussion time and frame, remember the following guidelines to have your best chance at resolving the conflict:

1. **Don't attack your partner.** Whenever people feel attacked, all they can do is defend themselves. Defensiveness leads to right-and-wrong arguing, black-and-white thinking, escalation of the argument, and hurt feelings. We have determined and experienced that this gets couples nowhere.

2. **Instead, talk about how you feel.** Talk about what was hard for you in the argument, how you felt angry, hurt, confused, or in despair. Talk about *yourself,* not your partner.

3. **Don't treat your partner as the enemy.** Put yourself in your partner's shoes and give him or her the benefit of the doubt. If you realize he or she is not hurting you on purpose, see how this changes your conversation.

4. **Tell your partner you love and value him or her.** You may be angry and/or hurt, *and* you still want to be close and find a resolution.

5. **Show your good intentions.** Talk instead about something you've learned about yourself; something new you have to say; or something you've thought of since the fight.

Don't repeat the same things that aren't working and have never worked when you've tried to resolve an argument. Do something different.

A Happy Resolution

Now that we've looked at the main obstacles that get in the way of a fruitful argument and set a few ground rules, let's look at an actual example of constructive conflict.

Stephanie and Trent had been living together for one year when they first came to see me. As usual I began by asking them what had brought them to my office. Like most couples, they had no trouble identifying the current conflict. And because they had been together for only a year, their first argument was very close at hand. It concerned housekeeping—and it was the same argument they were still having. To be brief: Trent thought Stephanie was a complete slob. "It's gotten so I can't invite anyone over," he said, "and I can barely stand to be in the house myself. I used to try and do all the cleaning, but it was a losing battle. I'd turn my back for a second, and there would be another pile of dirty laundry, old magazines, and unwashed dishes."

When Stephanie and Trent were home together, the atmosphere had become so pervasively tense that I felt I had to give them the one-week assignment of completely avoiding the issue of housekeeping. No matter how messy the house got, Trent was not permitted to say a word. No matter how disgusted Trent seemed, Stephanie was not permitted to say a word in self-defense.

Neither was permitted to clean the house. They were both instructed to simply observe their own reactions as the house grew messier and messier and be ready to talk about those reactions when next we met.

A week later they returned to my office. Trent didn't have a great deal to report, except that as the house grew messier he felt less able to perform the tasks of daily life. He couldn't find things, he couldn't make decisions, he couldn't get to work on time. But Stephanie had made a startling discovery. When she wasn't channeling her energy into resisting Trent's anger, she was able to understand something about her chronic untidiness that had until this time eluded her. Stephanie had grown up with a single mother who generally lived in a state of chaos. The only time her mother ever cleaned the house was when her boyfriend was coming over. In Stephanie's mind, cleaning house was associated with being a woman desperately trying to find and hold onto a man. As she was telling the story, she began to weep, and I could see how moved Trent was. Suddenly, and for the first time, he could see that Stephanie's sloppiness had nothing to do with an attempt to thwart him, and that it arose from something much deeper than her simply being messy.

The First Argument Technique revealed that at the root was a sad and frightened little girl who had always felt her mother neglected her—and the house—for her own needs. As Stephanie grew up, she was bound and determined not to repeat her mother's mistakes and subconsciously began to do the opposite: "I will not clean the house just to keep my man." Unfortunately, as with most people, the very defense mechanism that helped Stephanie survive her childhood (rebellion against her mother's actions) later blocked the growth and development needed for a healthy relationship. Stephanie looked at the fact that her refusal to keep the house clean was not only putting a wedge between her and Trent, but was also making her feel bad about herself. She was desperate to prove herself an independent woman, but she was going about it in the wrong way. She then began to disconnect the belief that being independent meant she had to be the opposite of her mother. Being independent actually meant she had to free herself of this childhood defense/survival structure so that she could choose how she wanted her house (and her life) to be and not be bound by reacting to her mother's choices. There is a big difference between choice and reaction, and Stephanie began to learn the difference. A clean house took on a whole new meaning. With this realization, Stephanie could finally begin to let go of the terrible shame she felt at being such a "slob" and allow herself to realize how much she really wanted to live in a clean and organized home.

Stephanie and Trent had been locked in the same repetitive argument for only a few months, but those were difficult months indeed. Paradoxically it required taking a step back from the argument to truly enter into it, to really see what was at stake. Once they did, the relief was almost immediate. Their story is a powerful example of how the very issue that we try so hard to avoid, the one we want to keep as far away from the wedding or the beginning of a relationship as possible, can actually bring about greater harmony and order once we truly invite the conflict in and address it. The conflict can actually help us create more intimacy and connection than if we shut it out.

Unfortunately many couples are afraid to delve so deeply at such an early phase of conflict. Cynthia and Allen, whose first argument occurred only days after their "perfect wedding" in Venice, didn't want to acknowledge the shadow that had entered their lives. Seven years later they realized they were still repeating the same lines. ("She's so demanding," he says. "He's always snapping at me," she says.) If only, like Stephanie and Trent, they'd been able to move directly to the source, they might have spared themselves the years of fruitless conflict.

In the next chapter, we'll discover the "hooks" that keep partners stuck in this hard, barren groove. And as we'll see, these same hooks can lead back to the place of true connection and fresh hope.

CHAPTER 2

Hooks—The Power of Patterns

Within the tenacity of the HOOK lies its healing power.

- A hook is the behavior of another person that provokes an intense and disproportionate reaction in
us.
- The hook points to the root of the problem within
each of us.
- The emotional attachment to the hook results from
the original hurt or trauma we experienced in our
past.
- The hook readily turns into a powerful, unconscious
pattern that is difficult to change.

In order to break the argument cycle, it is critical to
understand where the repetitive cycle begins. It starts
with getting *hooked*. A *hook* is the behavior of another
person that provokes an intense and disproportionate
reaction in us. For example, Mark's wife, Bernadette, had
the habit of parking her car in the driveway in such a
way that made it difficult for Mark to fit his own car next
to hers. He mentioned this to her many times, and Bernadette would always say she heard him, yet she never
parked her car differently. Mark couldn't understand
why she wouldn't move her car. He really began to get
angry when she kept agreeing that she'd change where
she parked the car yet never did. Because there never
was a resolution to this seemingly logistical issue, we
concluded that they were most likely hooked by something in their past. As it turned out, Mark felt that his

dad never took him seriously, and now he felt the same way whenever Bernadette ignored his request to park her car differently. Bernadette had a controlling mother who always told her what to do, so she rebelled by not moving her car, even though she understood that Mark's request wasn't even unreasonable.

Most of us know when we are having a strong reaction in an argument, but we simply don't understand and recognize that it's the disproportionate reaction to what our partner says or does that lets us know we're hooked, setting up the repetitive argument cycle. In order to change this strong reaction, you need to recognize when you're being hooked and what is hooking you.

Peeling Back the Hooks

Figuring out your hooks is a necessary component for beginning the peel process in the first of three steps of the First Argument Technique. You need to peel back the content of the argument, the subject matter that you are arguing about, in order to reveal (step two) the underlying issue from childhood, your story-below-the-story. This story-below-the-story causes your strong reaction and is simultaneously the ultimate source to healing yourself and your relationship. *Couples don't fight unless something in the present hooks them back to their unresolved issues from the past.* Once you discover your story-below-the-story, you can address the real issue behind the conflict and take the argument in a whole different direction. You can then talk about how you feel criticized or judged, rather than continue to argue about parking the car. You begin to shift your focus from the content issue to the inner feelings the argument has provoked.

As you will see in the following chapters and workbook, using all three steps of the First Argument Technique will give you the opportunity to turn your destructive fights into constructive arguments and conversations. Or, better yet, if you're reading this book at the first sign of conflict, you'll have the knowledge and tools necessary to *not* establish the patterns in the first place. As you read through this chapter, which fully describes all aspects of hooks, you will begin to understand the power of the first argument and its potential for healing.

"What's the big deal?" Lucas said. "Suit yourself." He uttered six words, and I was caught. I was under a spell of sorts. I was a grown woman in her backyard on a summer day in California, and I was a little girl called *Ug,* a girl who hadn't yet seen her real face in the mirror. The first step in peeling back the layer of a repetitive argument that has you hooked is to go to its root through the use of the First Argument Technique. From that root you will then be able to tap into its primal source within your own past.

What *Was* Your First Argument?

What if you can't remember your first argument? In my many years of experience, I've yet to encounter a couple who couldn't remember their first argument—no doubt because it tends to be painfully memorable. It may not be immediately accessible, but as you begin to review the history of the relationship, it floats to the surface. Usually one or both partners acknowledge that their current conflict did not spring up out of the blue. "This has been going on a long time," they tell me. When I ask, "Do you remember the first time you felt this way?" I am never met with a complete blank. Their versions of the "first time" may be slightly different. He'll say, "I made it clear that I didn't want to dance!" And she'll say, "No, you didn't!" But they both remember the incident. Even if it was not a spectacular blowup, it was the moment when something shifted, when the flow between them hit its first real snag. Often in remembering there's a certain disbelief. ("How could that honeymoon fight over a coconut cake be relevant fifteen years later?") But when they let go of their ideas about what should be relevant and *concentrate on the feelings they had at the time*— whether the feelings were of being ignored, dismissed, misunderstood, misled, criticized, mocked, abandoned, smothered, or betrayed—they recognize the incident as the template of their current struggle.

If, however, you and your partner really can't remember your first argument, don't worry. Start with whatever you can agree on as an early argument or with your most recent one. The whole point of this method is that the basic conflict repeats itself, in one form or another, until we acknowledge and resolve it. By all means don't distract yourselves with an argument over what your first argument was! And what about those couples who protest that they don't argue? If this is true for you, then just start with what you remember as your first disappointment.

One eighty-year-old woman told me that although she and her husband had never really had a full-fledged argument, she had a vivid memory of "when the first crack appeared." It was only a few weeks after their wedding, and she and her husband had just moved to a new city and settled into a tiny apartment. Her husband was a medical intern and spent long hours at the hospital. She was alone much of the time and did not yet have any local friends. One day, to relieve her loneliness and boredom, she threw herself into a plan to surprise her husband with a wonderful meal when he came home at the end of the day. Borrowing their landlady's pots and pans, she cooked a magnificent roast and baked her first pie. When her husband came home, she felt speechless with excitement. She waved her hand to indicate the beautifully set table, with its bouquet of flowers, opened bottle of wine, and two borrowed wine glasses. "What did you want to do all that for?" her husband said without more than a glance in her direction. And then, mumbling something about being too tired to eat, he went into the bedroom and promptly fell sound asleep. She didn't protest, and the incident was never spoken about, but it was a sad turning point in a brand-new marriage, and it remains a giant milestone in her memory.

So whether the first incident occurred with a bang or a whimper, the task is the same. As painful as it may be, try to reenter the scene of that first fall from grace, the moment you knew "the honeymoon was over," the moment your "perfect" partner and "perfect" relationship had a flaw. What words were spoken at that time? What gestures accompanied them? Did one person walk out of the room? Did a door slam? Did one person minimize or dismiss the other's intense reaction? Was there a sneer, a verbal put-down, a mocking laugh, or a cold glare? Usually at least one of these behaviors will evoke a particularly strong response for you. These behaviors are the hooks. They seize you and hold you. They are the behaviors you can't seem to stop, the ones you hold on to and "fight to the death" for because you feel as though your very survival depends on defending yourself and your position in the disagreement. Without even knowing it, these triggers are linked to your past. You know you're angry or hurt or disappointed, but you aren't exactly sure why. *You know you are hooked when one word or gesture stops you in your tracks and the rest of the conversation is lost.*

Where Does a Hook Come From?

A hook is a present-day happening that attaches to a deep vulnerability from the past. In most cases the roots of this vulnerability go back to childhood, to a specific traumatic event such as a death, abuse, or a divorce; a chronic condition, such as poverty or parental alcoholism; or simply the conflicts and disappointments that occur even within a relatively healthy family. For many people their relationship to one or both of their parents creates the template for intimate relationships in adulthood. For others, sibling relationships seem to be the most influential. No matter what our family background, to one degree or another, our personalities evolve in response to our perceptions of different events and behaviors from our childhood. Throughout our lives we remain susceptible to experiences that stir up this core vulnerability.

From a messy house to an unfinished fence, the "stirring" experience can appear quite trivial. But it holds power by connecting us to a site of constitutional weakness, a place where we have been wounded and rewounded. A lot of emotional energy is stored in such a place, and this energy supplies an argument with its heat and momentum.

The behaviors that hook you to your past are very powerful. They have the ability to take you out of the present moment and instantly transport you to a time when someone or something initially hurt you. For example, Beverly's partner, Jim, might say a phrase that's similar to or exactly what her father used to say to her—or the phrase may be completely different, but Jim's tone is the same as her dad used. At that point Jim has done something that has unwittingly triggered and hooked her. She's suddenly hurt and angry and is now telling Jim that he doesn't love her. Jim then defends himself, saying, of course, he loves her and just wishes she would close the garage door when she arrives home.

Once Beverly is hooked, her behavior and/or response is no longer related to what her husband just said; it's really about an issue that she had with her father, maybe even as long as twenty years ago. Neither Beverly nor Jim knows that Beverly just got hooked to a past event and suddenly was back in time, with feelings as vivid and strong as if she was still talking to her dad. This is the powerful phenomena of being hooked. We are hooked by a behavior that is familiar, and we remain hooked—responding as we did when the original wound occurred—until we (1) know we are hooked; (2) peel back from the hook; and (3) reveal to ourselves why we're hooked.

An argument tends to perpetuate itself with the same degree of intensity until the deep wound that fuels it has been seen and healed. This is bad news, for it means we are up against a powerfully conditioned behavior that is not likely to simply disappear on its own. Indeed the first incident of being hooked often turns into a pattern. But this self-perpetuating tendency is also good news, for it means that even the most frustrating and seemingly senseless conflict can provide direct access to a deep and important part of ourselves. In the very tenacity of a hook, we can glimpse at its potential healing power.

We can find a certain beauty, a kind of formal elegance, in the link between the first argument and the primal wound, because there is a profound paradox in the idea that something that hurts us (the primal wound) has the power to heal us once we discover it within our first argument. As the song goes, "The first cut is the deepest," *and it is the most lasting*. This lasting pain of the first "cut" is why the first argument within a relationship mirrors the original primal wound that occurred early in life. Once we are able to make use of this mirroring, it becomes possible to feel a measure of gratitude for the present conflict that opened our eyes to the past. Because of this link between present and past, we can find clarity and healing through a method as simple as the three-step First Argument Technique of peel, reveal, and heal.

Kinds of Hooks

Hooks often come in the form of words: *What's the big deal? Suit yourself.* Words are, in some ways, the easiest hooks to recognize. They tend to be more readily accessible to the conscious part of our minds, and we can write them down, free-associate to other words that have wounded us, and formulate alternative responses. However, it's also possible to be seized by a look or a gesture. One husband with whom I worked got hooked when his wife pointed a finger at him. His father used to shake his finger at him when he was a little boy, and the gesture always made him feel judged and ridiculed. My sixth-grade teacher often looked at me disapprovingly with her "sour look," as I called it. When I saw that look, it was as though my whole being constricted. I wanted to make myself small or invisible so the look couldn't find me. Still today it's easy for me to get hooked by a frown or simply by the absence of a smile.

Sometimes it's neither a look nor a gesture that seizes us but a more intangible dynamic, a certain mood, or a particular kind of ripple in the emotional atmosphere. Perhaps one man is hooked by the way his wife withdraws at a certain point in their interaction. Or his wife is hooked by her awareness of his mounting frustration—a frustration he doesn't give voice or gesture to, but which gets through to her nonetheless. For the couples who never argue, the hook is especially likely to come in a more subtle, nonverbal form.

For some people, however, it's what doesn't take place that hooks them. One woman told me that her first great disappointment with her husband occurred when he forgot an excursion they had planned together that she had eagerly anticipated. He just forgot—and she never said anything about it. Because her father had been ill throughout her childhood, she was used to having plans evaporate, longed-for occasions canceled, and holidays celebrated and vacations taken with the man of the family absent.

Though it may be more difficult initially to peel back and uncover a nonverbal hook, the process is essentially the same as with verbal hooks. As you would sift through sand with a metal detector, sift through your recurrent conflict, listening for the "buzz" that indicates heightened emotional intensity. As a therapist searching for a couple's hooks, I try to detect where the greatest charge occurs in their interaction, whether it's in the actual exchange or tone of words, a gesture, a welling of tears, or an intense moment of silence.

How Do We Know When We're Hooked?

We can't begin to get unhooked until we can recognize when we *are* hooked. This is not necessarily easy, since the essence of a hook is that it tends to bypass our conscious awareness. However, certain clues usually exist.

Intense, Uncontrollable Emotion

Perhaps the most important clue is that we drop out of conscious awareness. We feel a kind of fog descend or a sudden intensification of emotion. As if coming under a spell or repeating lines from a script, our behavior seems to become less and less voluntary. Although it's a little tricky to observe this moment in yourself, it's not impossible. It's like catching yourself in the moment when you're about to fall asleep at the wheel or take the sip of wine that's going to send you over the line between slightly giddy and truly drunk. Unfortunately it's not possible to set a mechanical alarm to sound the moment you're being hooked. Simply intending to be alert to that moment, however, can function as a mental alarm of sorts. The hardest thing, of course, is to catch a hook for the first time. But once you've brought a hook into consciousness, it's as though you've injected it with a colored dye and thereafter it becomes much easier to spot.

From the moment I sat down and scribbled those phrases in my Fourth of July glossary, I was much less susceptible to being snagged by them. In any case, one thing that can be said about a hook is this: If you miss it the first time, you can be sure that it will come around again and give you another chance to deal with it!

Seemingly Irrational Arguments
Another clue that we're getting hooked is that the charge we feel around a certain interaction is disproportionate to its surface content. A disagreement about a fence feels as significant as the partition of Jerusalem; a conflict over where to put the wastepaper basket takes on the intensity of a child-custody battle. To recognize that the charge is disproportionate is not to dismiss the significance of what's at stake. It's quite the opposite. But it's not until we defuse the charge, by bringing more awareness to the interaction, that we have any hope of understanding what is at stake and why.

Exaggerating the Issue
Another clue closely related to irrational arguments is that we take a single, specific issue—a messy house, for

example—as proof of something big. We say things such as "This relationship will never work," "Nobody ever listens to me," or "I never get what I want in life." Although it's true that little things can be important signs about a person's character and the viability of a relationship, it's hard to distinguish a *sign* from a *hook* until we've learned to recognize the latter. We'll return to this subject later.

Hooks and Arrows

The feeling of being hooked in an argument can strongly resemble the feeling of suddenly falling in love. Even though the latter is pleasant and the former is not, the two are actually quite similar. Both often carry the sense of a disproportionate charge. We feel much more intense about someone or something than the situation warrants. Though we may not be able to put our finger on it, we have a sense of something that feels deeply familiar. And finally, we have the sense of being compelled, of being pulled in a way that falls outside our rational control.

The structural similarity between falling in love and being hooked is not coincidental. For indeed what often draws us most powerfully to another person is the recognition—whether conscious or unconscious—that he or she will tap into our deepest vulnerability. One of my friends tells the story of being in the bookstore where she worked and seeing a coworker buy *The Well Body Book*. She found herself thinking, "Maybe he has headaches!" And in one instant this thought became, "I'm in love with him!" Her father had always suffered from terrible headaches, and in believing she was falling in love with a man who also had chronic health problems, she was forcibly yanked by her primal need to rescue a man and make him well. Cupid's arrow pierced her in the exact same place that, later, when she did indeed become involved with the *Well Body* man, would become the source of ongoing conflict.

Falling in love is so pleasurable that we feel little motivation to examine the deep vulnerability that may lie at the root of it. We simply want to perpetuate the spell, to hold onto the mysterious feeling of having found the one who knows the secret combination that opens the door to our most primal longing for love and approval. For many couples, it's not until a painful conflict has become unbearably chronic or acute that they find the willingness to face old wounds and begin the difficult work of healing them.

Why Do We Get Hooked?

Hooks have a magnetic power. We are drawn to the words and behaviors that hook us. We are also drawn to hook our loved ones in the places where they are most vulnerable.

It often seems that deep inside a couple's initial attraction lies the subconscious recognition of how to hook and be hooked. Sometimes the fit can be all too perfect. In a poem of Margaret Atwood's, she refers to men and women fitting together perfectly the way a hook fits into an eye.

The cynical view of such a "perfect" fit is that, as in certain preying animals, pure aggression drives us to sense each other's Achilles heel and sink our teeth in at precisely that point. A less cynical but still pessimistic view is that we are so powerfully drawn to the familiar that we are more or less doomed to recreate, in adult life, the same negative patterns that formed us in childhood.

A more positive perspective, and the one that I choose to believe is true, is that each of us is drawn to heal our own greatest weakness and—often without consciously knowing why—choose a partner who can help us in this task. Much to our dismay this help may arrive in the form of a painful conflict that we get swept into again and again.

Eli and Amber, a couple in their early thirties, came to me in their fifth year of marriage. They had been high school sweethearts; Amber had fallen in love with Eli's kindness and generosity, and Eli was drawn to Amber's devotion to her friends and family and her determination to succeed in her career. Over time, however, the very qualities that Eli admired in Amber became problematic. Amber's mother was disabled and lived with the young couple, along with Amber's younger sisters, making it difficult for Eli and Amber to ever have time alone together. Meanwhile, Amber began to work especially hard at a new management job, had a long drive to and from the city every day, and was consumed with her work. She and Eli had little time together during the week, and on weekends, when she wasn't catching up with her work, she was often collapsed in a state of exhaustion. When Eli pleaded with Amber to make some changes in her schedule, he felt she reacted defensively, without really listening to him. Discouraged, he began spending more and more time with one of his coworkers. Eventually the two had an affair. Despite the intensity of his conflicting emotions, Eli knew that he loved Amber and wanted to save their marriage. Before the affair had gone on for very long, he told Amber about it, and they immediately came for therapy.

As always, that first day I asked them if they remembered their first argument. They did. Not long after they married, Amber had wanted her mom and two younger sisters to move in with them. Eli wanted them to be close by, but not in the same house. Their first argument involved Eli's resentment around these issues. Because

Eli truly was a kind, generous man, and he prided himself on these qualities, he felt guilty about his resentment and did not sit down to address the issues with Amber directly. Instead he would intermittently blow up at her for being so unavailable. At these points Amber would become defensive about her family and her career. Round and round they went with this repetitive argument, which never got any closer to being resolved.

Using steps one and two of the First Argument Technique, we explored the first conflict a bit further. It emerged that Amber had been operating out of her childhood pattern of feeling solely responsible for everything that happened in her family. Having grown up with a father who criticized her no matter how hard she tried, Amber had never been able to believe that she was a good and successful person. Always trying to prove herself to her father, even long after he had left the family and moved away, Amber had become the classic workaholic.

Eli had grown up with an excessively close relationship with his mother. That relationship could tolerate little conflict or disagreement, and Eli moved from boyhood to manhood with the belief that he had to be "a good boy" or "a nice guy" all the time. From the beginning of his marriage to Amber, he had colluded with her excessive sense of responsibility—allowing her family to live with them, accepting her compulsive work habits—until it finally became unbearable.

Thus the acute problem that brought them into my office—Eli's affair—had its roots in the dynamic that was present in their very first argument. Because of his own fused relationship with his mother, Eli had been attracted by Amber's independence. Yet at the same time, he wanted to be the center of attention, as he had been for his extremely doting mother. His perpetual disappointment with Amber recreated her primal sense of never being able to please her father. Once again we see that the particular hooks that catch each partner in an intimate relationship are reinforced by the deep magnetism that first drew them together. Along with the lack of awareness that tends to surround a hook, this primal pull is another significant reason why a hook so readily turns into a pattern.

A situation like Eli and Amber's reveals another powerful advantage of the First Argument Technique. When Eli and Amber came to see me, they were in crisis. The affair was so recent, the wounds so raw, that the process of talking with each other about the situation was almost impossible. Putting the affair on the back burner in those first few sessions gave us a calmer, more neutral atmosphere within which to work. By peeling back the current issue, we were able to bypass a great deal of intense, polarized emotion and to arrive—quickly—at the roots of their struggle, revealing the deeper wounds that needed healing.

Why Not Just "Let Go"?

Sometimes people ask me, "Once you've identified a hook and have understood why you get hooked, can't you just let it go?" I tell them that letting go is much easier said than done. Too often what masks as letting go is really a form of resignation. The eighty-year-old woman who had cooked the beautiful supper for her husband told me, "I'd spent all day preparing that meal. When he turned away from me without even tasting one bite, something inside me shut down. In that moment, I decided that I would never put myself out for him in that way again. And I didn't." The two of them went on to have a stable and relatively peaceful marriage that lasted fifty-five years. Some people might say, "Why ask for more?" My response is that while this young wife avoided the turmoil of conflict with her husband, she also cut them both off from the possibility of moving through conflict to a richer form of intimacy. How sad that this young wife squelched, from that day forward, her yearning to surprise her husband with a burst of her naturally generous and creative energy. How sad that her young husband was never again greeted by such a surprise.

I tell my clients that there are two sure ways to stunt, maim, or perhaps even kill a relationship. One is to stay locked in perpetual conflict; the other is to give up in resignation. People often give up without trying because they feel helpless to change the other person. They fail to understand that the other person might be able to change if given a chance. Sometimes when a disappointment is aired and heard, there can be significant relief and a radical deepening of intimacy even if the other person doesn't change. And most important, it's not really about changing the other person but rather about changing oneself. The core of the First Argument Technique is that each of us is responsible for healing ourselves by looking in our own mirror.

Expressing Disappointment Can Foster Intimacy

A client of mine, Sonya, is in a relatively new relationship. She told me about a conversation she recently had with her partner, Nicholas, that she felt was significant.

I'm a very verbal person, and Nicholas just isn't. He's very physically affectionate, he's very generous, and he shows his love for me in many very tangible ways that I truly do appreciate. But every now and again I feel the need for some sort of verbal reassurance or confirmation.

I just need him to tell me, in a sentence or two, what it is he likes about me and about us! It's hard for me to come right out and ask for what I want, because I'm very aware that I'm fishing for a compliment. So I tend to throw out these rather subtle little verbal "balls" to him, which he doesn't pick up.

The feeling of disappointment had been building up in me for several weeks already when, the other day, it happened. We were sitting together on the sofa, and I made one of my little verbal overtures. Instead of responding, he reached out and picked up a joke book that was lying on the coffee table and started reading me a joke. This time I didn't let it go. I said to him, "Are you aware that we're having one of those Men-Are-from-Mars-Women-Are-from-Venus *moments?" He blushed and said, "Sort of." And then I just started to talk to him, without blame, about what it was I sometimes longed for and why. As I was telling him these things, I felt that he was truly listening to me. Afterwards I realized that I didn't know if he would ever be able to really change his behavior—it's such a stretch for him. I imagine it would be as if I, having never been particularly limber or coordinated, were to suddenly try to do gymnastics. But just the fact that I expressed myself and felt truly heard by him has made a big difference for me.*

What would have happened in the moment that Nicholas picked up the joke book if, rather than expressing her longing as she did, Sonya had simply "stuffed it"? The image I like to use is this: If Sonya, like the young doctor's wife, had decided to close and seal the lid on her disappointment, it would have been as though a door shut on a room within the "house" of their relationship. Nicholas might not have known exactly what was in that room, but because Sonya, like most people, would probably not have been able to maintain an airtight seal on the door, over time he would have come to feel her disappointment as something clouding the atmosphere.

In communicating her disappointment and feeling heard, it's as though Sonya changed the locked door on that room into a gauze curtain. Now Nicholas can see what's behind that curtain and has a chance to try to do something about it. Even if he is not ultimately able to transform himself into the fountain of verbal affirmation that Sonya might wish for, the fact that he can see and acknowledge her wish will create more intimacy between them. Any intimate relationship includes certain places where we cannot fully meet the other's needs. However, if we can see and name these places without blame, we don't feel so isolated and closed off.

As for Eli and Amber, they certainly exemplify the value of courageously facing a conflict. Moving through their current crisis to its first manifestation, they were able to not only acknowledge one another's frustrated needs and desires, but also make accommodations in their behavior. In the course of therapy, they were both able to examine their old patterns and begin to see that their own self-worth was not entirely dependent on self-sacrifice. This brought them great relief as individuals, and it brought them closer together as a couple. It took several years for them to fully rebuild their trust in one another, but gradually they did. Amber found a job closer to home, and, while she continued to be a devoted daughter to her ailing mother, she and Eli moved into their own house.

It's never pleasant to be hooked into a recurrent conflict with the person with whom we once felt so in love. Yet without a painful conflict, most of us probably would not find the determination to face our childhood wounds, which will undoubtedly surface at one time or another, and discover a new level of intimacy with one another. For many of us, the early wounding took place at a core, preverbal level, so we don't even realize what we're really fighting about. It's not until we find ourselves unable to express our feelings during a conflict that we realize we need to access this preverbal information to understand our fight.

What remains unconscious will return in the form of repetitive conflict. This is a truism in psychology, and it is a cornerstone of the First Argument Technique. Until we bring the light of consciousness to bear on the root of our repetitive conflicts, these conflicts will, in spite of our good intentions and best efforts to stop them, arise again and again.

Did Amber fall in love with Eli because deep down she suspected that through the pain of their relationship she might be forced to heal her most painful childhood wound? Who can really say? Adopting this positive explanation for the mystery of attraction is not the most important thing. The one belief that is essential to anyone who really wants to create a healthy relationship is this: *It is up to me whether a conflict becomes a painful groove or a movement toward growth.* If you are ready to make this statement with at least some degree of conviction, then you are ready to take the next step and learn how to unhook.

CHAPTER 3

Unhooking with the Story-below-the-Story

Changing one small thing in your repetitive pattern will begin to change the whole pattern automatically. Baby steps count! They are the beginning of UNHOOKING and changing.

- Identifying the first argument is a powerful way to cut through an entrenched current conflict.
- The surface issue of the current conflict can be deceptively compelling.
- When we unhook from the surface issue, we can find the story-below-the-story that is the real source of conflict and pain.
- The story-below-the-story is the key to healing. Whenever we feel hooked into our recurrent conflict, the story-below-the-story can help us drop down to a deeper layer of intimacy.
- Handling one another's story-below-the-story with care is crucial. Each person's story-below-the-story is a revelation of deep vulnerability and should not be used as a weapon.
- The story-below-the-story helps us change the present while addressing, yet not dwelling in, the past.

Clare and Jeremy, a couple in their thirties who'd been married ten years, came into my office for the first time. I began with my usual question: "What brings the two of you here today?" They both looked deeply embarrassed, a bit like children who'd been sent to the principal's office, and there was a pause before they managed to tell me that they had come because they were fighting constantly "over the dumbest things."

"Like what?" I asked.

"Well," Clare said, "if you can believe it, the latest was about cookies!" She looked at me as though I might fall out of my chair, but when I didn't, she continued. "Our daughter and I made cookies the other day. Some were for the family, and some were for Jeremy to take to work. I was very clear with Jeremy about which were which, but somehow he managed to not hear me, and he took almost all the cookies to work. I was furious and hurt."

Jeremy had his own story. He had wanted to be sure he took enough cookies so that everyone in his office could have some. It seemed to him that he'd left plenty for the house, and he didn't think Clare would mind much if he took a few extra to work. Though Jeremy apologized to her, he was stunned at her reaction. "It's only cookies!" he told her. "How could you be so upset?" Clare, too, seemed genuinely perplexed. She knew that her distress was disproportionate to a handful of cookies (the hook), but she also knew that her distress was very real.

Creating a Safe Space

From the moment they walked in, Clare and Jeremy had some awareness that the "dumb things" they were arguing about were not the whole story. As intense as the cookie argument had been, they both knew that the cookies themselves weren't the real issue; there was a deeper layer waiting to be revealed. For many couples, however, the most recent argument is not so transparent. As we saw in Chapter 1 with the young couple who battled over housekeeping, the current struggle can be overpowering. Stephanie and Trent had been deadlocked over their messy house, and the only way to break it was to declare a temporary truce. For one week, as they lived side by side, they agreed to stay mum on the subject of housecleaning. Free from the distraction of the ongoing conflict, Stephanie was able to make the remarkable discovery about her horror of housekeeping.

For many couples, a truce is actually the first step in unhooking. Such a truce is often necessary in order to step back and see the hooks, rather than simply get snagged by them. This is why I ask couples who are entrenched in a particular conflict or state of tension to give each other a week's break. During this time, they promise to avoid their triggering issues. If, after the first week, nothing has yet bubbled to the surface, then I ask them to refrain from stirring things up for another week, and so on. Occasionally people complain that they feel as though they're being superficial or practicing denial, but I explain to them that they're creating a kind of psychic oasis so that the underlying source of their conflict can emerge. For most couples, a week is more than sufficient, and some, like Clare and Jeremy, don't require such a time-out at all.

Finding the Links

When Clare and Jeremy arrived at my door, they were already asking themselves, "What's really going on when we're fighting about cookies?" In their case, I felt we could immediately try steps one and two of the First Argument Technique: peel away the surface issue to reveal the bridge to the deeper layer. I asked Clare, "What do you think really got to you when you woke up that morning and discovered the missing cookies?" She thought for a moment and answered, "It's the feeling that he didn't listen to me, that somehow my words don't count."

"And what about the first argument you ever had as a couple?" I asked her. "Can you remember?" She did, and Jeremy remembered it, too. At a party, before they were married, Clare noticed that another woman was paying a lot of attention to Jeremy. Jeremy not only seemed to be enjoying the attention, he was responding in a way that made Clare feel invisible. When Clare erupted on the way home, Jeremy told her that he had just been being friendly and that she was "making something out of nothing."

What was the link between the cookies and the party? In both instances, Clare felt as though something that properly belonged to her, within the sphere of their intimate relationship, was being shared with others. Jeremy violated Clare's sense of boundaries. Furthermore, Clare did not feel fully taken into account by Jeremy. Her "something" was turned into a "nothing." She felt unheard and unseen, which was a feeling that had permeated her childhood experience within her family. This is the place where Clare gets hooked in her confrontations with Jeremy.

Jeremy on the other hand had been orphaned at a young age and then taken into foster care. He has a hard time feeling he genuinely belongs anywhere, and so he works hard—bestowing his attention, bestowing cookies—to make himself feel accepted by others. When Clare chastises him for what she feels is his inappropriate generosity, he gets hooked in his place of deepest vulnerability. Within moments he is back in the orphanage, in a condition of scarcity.

Oddly enough this link to a well of painful memories was a great relief to Clare and Jeremy. For now they could see that they'd been having the same argument over and over and that no matter how trivial its surface issue might be, it was about something that mattered deeply to each of them. Rather than overwhelming the couple, this realization released them from a sense of fruitlessness and frustration. Now they had a powerful insight into the root of their struggle.

The Story-below-the-Story

Over the years I have come to believe that recognizing the story-below-the-story (also referred to as the "core issue") is the key to intimacy. Because the story-below-the-story is the root cause of intimate conflict, it is the key to determining what is getting in the way of intimacy with your partner. Without knowing your core issue, negative fighting patterns develop and continue throughout your relationship. Any number of techniques exist for addressing negative patterns of interaction, but if we don't get to the root of these patterns, we stay at a relatively superficial level, providing only symptomatic relief.

Fortunately it is not so difficult for most people to uncover the primal layer of the story. Why? Because it is such a powerful story, lying at the core sense of self and, in different versions, replaying itself over and over. Except in cases of serious childhood trauma, where the need to repress can overwhelm awareness, I rarely meet people who cannot find their way back to their own story-below-the-story. It does help to have some simple guidelines, however.

The First Argument Technique

Step One: Peel
Locating the Hook and Deciphering
Your First Argument
As we saw in the previous chapter, *the first step starts with locating the hook in your current argument*—whether

56

verbal ("What's the big deal?"), nonverbal (a look, a gesture, an emotional withdrawal), or situational (as when she wants to dance but he doesn't, or he wants a clean house but she's messy).

Continue by returning to the scene of your very first argument as a couple. This move defuses the charge around the current issue even as it reminds us that the current issue is linked to a primal core feeling (from childhood) and, therefore, significant. (Again, if you're one of the rare couples for whom the first argument is truly shrouded in mist, then simply go back to an earlier incarnation of the current conflict.)

Once you've retrieved the earlier argument and peeled away the content of the argument (i.e., the cookies), ask yourself, "What's the recurrent pattern here?" With Clare and Jeremy, the recurrent pattern—the place where each of them got hooked—involved his need for attention and her feeling of being unseen and unheard. It also involved divergent views as to what belongs in the "inner circle" and what belongs "outside" of their own personal boundaries. Since Jeremy never had a family that was truly his own, his sense of boundary is much looser than Clare's, which, in turn, stirs up her insecurities.

The First Argument Technique

Step Two: Reveal
Uncovering the Story-below-the-Story

From this core dynamic, drop down to reveal the story-below-the-story. Remember that you're looking for either a painful incident and/or a repeated pattern from childhood. Sometimes—as in my own case—you will initially feel that the material is just out of reach, on the tip of the tongue. When trying to reveal the story-below-the-story, I tell my clients, "Just keep patiently asking your-self, 'Have I ever felt this way before? When? What was going on at the time?'"

Some people find it helpful to ask this question before going to sleep and as soon as possible upon awakening. This prompts our less conscious, less controlling self to sift through the material during the night, often yielding an insight the next morning. Jotting down dreams in a notebook kept close by the bed also helps in the process. For example, a young woman named Nicole dreamed that her boyfriend had taken her to a crummy diner where the coffee tasted like rusty water. Writing down the dream she remembered an incident shortly after her father had left her mother. Wanting to cheer her mother up, Nicole had taken her out to a little cafe. Her mother had taken one sip of coffee and announced, "This coffee tastes like rusty water!" Making the connection between the dream and her parents' divorce helped Nicole to understand that at the crux of her current ongoing conflict was the fear that her boyfriend, like her father, would leave.

Free-associating in a journal is another powerful tech-nique, as I learned for myself on that momentous Fourth of July when I reached for the nearest scrap of paper. Assuming you're in less rugged circumstances than I was, take out a sheet of paper and jot down a quick descrip-tion of your most recent argument, for example, "messy house" or "missing cookies." Think about the words your partner spoke in anger; record those that were most painful to you: "You're just so lazy!" or "It's only cook-ies!" Was there a pointing finger, a dismissive shrug, or a frowning face that really got to you? What did you feel when you heard these words or witnessed that gesture or expression? Allow that feeling to rise. Stay with it for a while. Then, using the phrase "I remember . . .," begin writing. Don't think about what you're going to write, just write. When a memory comes—"I remember my brother looking at me with his taunting face"—write down everything that accompanies the memory. It doesn't have to be an elaborate description. A simple list will do, as in, "The dining room. Mother's Chinese vase. The mirror on the wall . . ." When that memory seems to run dry, begin again with "I remember . . ."

Another helpful phrase to use is, "The truth about . . ." For example, "The truth about my not cleaning the house is . . .," "The truth about taking those cookies to work is . . .," or "The truth about my relationship is . . ." People are often surprised at what comes bubbling up to finish the sentence. Yet another strong opener is, "What would happen if . . . ?" For instance, "What would happen if I allowed myself to dance?" "What would happen if I didn't take what he was saying personally?" These questions, I've found, are extremely effective for tapping into a core belief, such as, "If I allow myself to dance, I'll make a fool of myself," "If I allow myself to dance, she'll see how insecure I am," or "If I didn't take what was being said by my partner personally, maybe that would mean I don't love him." These phrases actually tap into our deepest fears and belief system.

A written dialogue with yourself can help to reveal the story-below-the-story. You might try to give yourself two names. For example, Stephanie of the messy house might have written the following dialogue:

STEPHANIE: *Why don't you like to clean the house?*
STEPH: *I just don't.*
STEPHANIE: *Come on, Steph. There must be some reason.*
STEPH: *I don't want to talk about it. Stop bothering me!*
STEPHANIE: *Whatever, you know I'm right! You're such a mess. I'm going to tell Mom.*

STEPH: *Mom? What does she care? She only cleans the house when her boyfriend is coming over.*

If you find it hard to write a dialogue, try simply having a dialogue with your two hands. It may sound childish, but, in fact, that's the point! We're trying to move through the layers of adult personas to find the old wound in the very young self. A dialogue between "Righty" and "Lefty" might be exactly the pathway that's needed.

Yet another way to retrieve early material is through drawing. Without worrying about artistic merit, try drawing some familiar childhood settings in as much detail as possible—for example, your childhood bedroom, the kitchen in your childhood home, the barn at your grandma's house, and so forth. The very act of drawing—especially if you use materials that are reminiscent of childhood, such as crayons on fairly large sheets of newsprint or oatmeal paper—can help cut through the layers of learned behavior, defenses, and hurts that have occurred since childhood. It's amazing how much information will be revealed by drawing, rather than talking.

Sometimes, when people insist they're "totally blocked" and "just can't remember anything" about their childhood, I encourage them to spend some time looking through old photo albums. Find one or two photographs that seem especially evocative of your early life. If possible, take them out and put them up someplace where you will see them several times each day. One woman found a photograph of herself at age three and placed it on top of her dresser. In the photograph she is sitting slumped over on a sofa and her face looks sad and smudged. "I always used to call it my 'rotten egg picture,'" she said, "though I never really knew why. The photograph was taken a few days after my father left the family. Suddenly one morning I realized that grief and a feeling of being ugly have always been linked for me." This realization helped her to understand her extreme sensitivity to anything her husband might say about her appearance—the issue that fueled their repetitive conflict.

Whatever technique you feel drawn to use, the key is to stay with the predominant feeling that accompanies your recurrent argument. Even if at first you don't have a name for this feeling and can't put words to it, don't worry. Just feel it in your body: the lump in your throat, the dread in your belly, the tightness in your chest, the impulse to flee or to hide. After many years of using this approach with couples, I can say with confidence that if you simply allow the feeling to rise and linger for a few moments each day, it will lead you back to its source.

Once you've made the link and peeled the conflict to reveal the story-below-the-story, continue to stay with it awhile. Allow other memories to gather around it, and take some time to absorb its implications before immediately spilling it out to your partner. The impulse to blurt can be powerful, but I encourage people to save that impulse for a journal or sketchbook. It's already a big event for your psyche to retrieve such a memory. You don't need to also immediately absorb your partner's reaction to it. After several days, when you've allowed the story to settle inside you and you feel truly ready to share it, remember to do so without blame.

Avoid saying, "You're doing the same thing to me that my brother always did!" Instead explain, "Now I understand why I get so upset when you say, 'You're too sensitive.'"

For the majority of couples with whom I have worked, the very revelation of the story-below-the-story significantly defuses the charge around the current issue. Nina and David were a couple in their fifties who had been married for twenty years. When they first came to see me, David had just moved out because they couldn't come to an agreement about "fairness" in the relationship. Each felt that the other did not contribute enough to the household chores, and neither felt seen, heard, or validated. They had been going around and around with this feeling of inequity for years, to the point that each had drawn up a flowchart to prove "I am doing more than you!" Much to their disappointment, even the flowcharts, though very detailed, did not put an end to the argument. All that seemed to be coming to an end was the relationship itself. Both of them expressed to me that they could not go on any longer with things as they were.

I asked about their first argument. They agreed that it occurred on the day they got back from their honeymoon. Although they both had excellent jobs at the time, it had suddenly become obvious to Nina that David wanted to have kids right away and that he had pictured her as a stay-at-home mom. This was not Nina's vision for herself, and she was starting to see a domineering side of David that she hadn't sensed before. Nina came from a family that stressed equality, and she had always valued her job and her ability to make a good living. David admitted having received a "macho" upbringing from both his father and grandfather, but he insisted that he had fallen in love with Nina partly for her independent spirit.

When their first conflict arose, they had no idea how to resolve their different timelines for having children. David felt Nina was stalling and would never decide to have kids, and Nina felt David was pressuring her. In over twenty years they had never resolved these basic issues of whose needs were more important than whose, and a lot of resentment had built up between them. Nina felt the only way she had power in the relationship was to resist David's goals, and David felt the only way he had power was to periodically leave. Since they had been given no tools to work with, their flowcharts were a desperate attempt to regulate their turbulent relationship.

By the end of that first session I made them throw away their flowcharts, and I explained to them that we needed to go deeper, to find the story-below-the-story. It didn't take long for them to see that their conflict revolved around power and equality and to discover why this conflict held such power for each of them. As a child, David had often felt overwhelmed by the domineering force of his father and grandfather. He had grown into an adult who needed to assert his own authority. Nina had grown up with a fierce drive toward self-determination, with a tremendous fear of being thwarted, of becoming a dependent wife. They had both agreed that Nina would, therefore, go back to work soon after their child was born. This situation was exacerbated when they had twins, and Nina had to stay home with them longer than she had planned. She was frustrated and resentful that she couldn't resume her independent lifestyle. David felt resentful that all the pressure was on him to work longer hours to support the family and that he had to do chores at home too. This led to the creation of flowcharts to see who really was doing more than the other.

As they began to truly listen to each other, Nina and David began to have compassion for each other, to acknowledge one another's longings and feelings of being overwhelmed with their twins. Rather than haggling over flowcharts, they started trying to actually change their behavior toward each other. When Nina feels like stalling, she has begun to talk about her feelings of being pressured by David's timelines. When David fears that precious time is being lost, he has started to look at his own anxieties rather than bolting out the door. He has realized that his pattern of leaving has been hurtful to Nina and has never resolved anything between them.

They are both exploring new ways of feeling powerful within themselves, rather than blaming the other.

Changing the Patterns

With Nina and David I was able to see, once again, the sadness and fear that lie at the bottom of most recurrent arguments. Each time I witness such a moment, it renews my faith in the fundamental innocence—the hurt child—that waits at the root of most human conflict. In this way, the story-below-the-story acts as a guide, bringing us back to the deep truth whenever we get lost in the thicket of day-to-day hurts, disappointments, and misunderstandings.

Of course, as with any entrenched habit, even when you've located the source of its intensity, the recurrent argument isn't likely to magically disappear. Once you've cleared the path to the story, it's important to keep that path clear by weeding out the scraggly underbrush of bad habits that we discussed earlier. Avoid blaming, shaming, and name-calling. Try to let go of the compulsion to be right. Above all, remember that each partner's story-below-the-story must be handled with care. By definition it involves the revelation of a great personal vulnerability, and it should never be used to humiliate the other. ("Poor little foster boy, always wanting his mommy!") Nor should it be used to dismiss the current conflict. ("You're not really upset that I'm going away for a month, you're just reliving the trauma of your childhood abandonment!") To use the story-below-the-story as a weapon would be a significant betrayal and a major setback. I myself have come to see it as a kind of sacred revelation, worthy of the highest respect.

Now, when the old patterns exert their pull, you have a touchstone to bring you back. You're not so likely to get caught in the surface disturbance of a messy house, a missing batch of cookies, or an unbuilt fence. Once you've gained a certain confidence in your ability to resist these patterns, it's time to take the next big step and create some new patterns of interaction.

First Argument Technique

Step Three: Heal
New Patterns of Verbal Response:
Getting beyond Defensiveness

As we've seen, an argument usually involves a highly charged exchange of words. In a recurrent argument, couples tend to repeat certain words in an almost ritualistic way. Thus far we've learned how to recognize which of these highly charged words are hooks and to understand why they carry such power for us. For some people this process alone will alter the pattern of verbal exchange. Most of us, however, will need to actually practice some different responses.

"What's the big deal?" Lucas exclaimed when I expressed disappointment over the fence. For me, because I'd learned not to trust my own perceptions, these words triggered a defensive pattern of angry surrender. I'd stutter a bit, then throw up my hands—but without letting go of the resentment. On that same Fourth of July evening, after writing down the words that tended to hook me, I also wrote down some alternate responses.

"Well, it is a big deal to me!" was one such response. And I realized that if I'd been able to say these words without shame or fury, they might have led to a real conversation rather than the standoff that was our typical outcome. For example, I might have gone on to explain why it was a big deal, in a way that didn't threaten Lucas.

"You have a real gift for knowing what I want, so when I think you've promised me something and it doesn't happen, I feel very disappointed."

Defensive responses take on many different forms: Some people immediately back off, some lash out, and others move into evasiveness or denial. As different as these responses are, what they have in common is that each, in its own way, puts an end to true conversation. Once we've gone into a defensive mode, we're no longer really listening to the other person. We're attending to our own hurt, trying to build a wall around it, trying to ward off further injury.

The first step, then, in changing the pattern of response is to recognize what sort of defensive reaction you tend to have. If you can't immediately do so, then think back to your most recent argument. Once you felt hooked, how did you react? What did you say? What did you do? Partners are usually all too familiar with each other's defensive moves. So when you're not in the midst of an argument, use each other's knowledge to help fill in the blanks. Remember to do so for the sake of understanding—not in order to get in a dig or add more fuel to the fire.

Once you feel you've identified your pattern, try out some alternate responses. For instance, if your pattern (like mine) is a form of angry surrender, then it's important to practice staying engaged. Hang in there, hold your ground—but without condemnation of the other. For the person whose pattern is to evade or deny conflict, the antidote is similar: Don't drop the ball. Acknowledge that a problem exists. Using I statements, speak about yourself, how you feel, and explain what's hard for you. Practice using the words "I feel," so you don't just shut down and ignore the conflict.

If your defensive pattern is blaming, then it's especially important to use I statements. An I statement is a way to report your own feelings as accurately as possible ("It's really hard for me to function in a messy house"), rather than to make a judgment of the other person by blaming ("You're such a slob!"). The value of such messages is that they allow you to express yourself and to impart significant information (i.e., what's hard for you) about a conflict in a way that your partner can really hear and absorb.

For example, if I am hurt by something my partner has just said, I could make the following I statement: "I was really hurt by what you just said and actually stopped listening to you." A you statement (i.e., blaming statement) would sound like this: "You always say things to hurt me. You're really mean to me, and I'm ending the conversation now until you can apologize to me for the awful things you said." The I statement tells your partner that you got hurt, and it also tells him that you stopped listening. These are all things that happened for you, which if you don't tell him, he might never know. The you statement places blame on your partner, making it all his fault without telling him how you feel and what happens for you when you feel that way. When you use an I statement in an argument, there is a chance for resolution because you're taking responsibility for your feelings and not just telling your partner he has to change, apologize, and so on. The I statement invites a person to participate in a dialogue with you. The you statement creates defensiveness in both partners. When you're busy defending yourself and your position, it's almost impossible to resolve an argument, because your energy is going into defending rather than talking and resolving.

I statements can be misused, however, and it's important to stay alert to a false I statement that is really a covert attack. "It hurts my feelings when you're so dishonest" or

"I feel really upset when you manipulate me." Such statements may be framed as I messages, but they are actually powerful negative judgments of the other person. Fortunately, when we tap into the story-below-the-story, there is a natural movement toward authentic I statements. Having uncovered the foster boy or the girl whose mother only cleaned house for her boyfriends, we simply become much less interested in criticizing our partners. Techniques can be valuable, but it's especially gratifying when a negative pattern of interaction is changed via a genuine shift in perception.

In changing our patterns of verbal communication, the goal is to be true to ourselves in a way that creates greater intimacy with our partner. When Clare says, "It really hurt my feelings when so many of the cookies were gone, because I felt like I wasn't being heard," she accomplishes this goal. Rather than simply dismissing her own distress ("It's only cookies!"), she enables Jeremy to understand the source of her distress, and she in turn is better able to understand that his action was not so much a dismissal of her as it was a reaction to his own painful story.

It's wonderful to realize that self-expression and deeper companionship are not contradictory—indeed, with awareness, they are deeply complementary.

New Patterns of Behavior

Many of us have patterns of response that originated in early childhood experiences. These patterns are not so much verbal as behavioral: We fly into a rage, we withdraw into a sulk and punish with a cold silence, or we collapse in despair. These patterns, deeply ingrained in the body, can be hard to change, so we need to be patient—both with ourselves and our partners.

Rage

For obvious reasons, the pattern of quickly escalating to rage is the most dangerous of all. We risk saying terrible things to those we love most, and, at the extreme, we risk doing actual physical damage. Those who habitually give way to rage risk losing their love and work relationships, and, more significantly, they risk permanently damaging their children. To avoid the consequences of impulsive rage, it is crucial to take a time-out. A recommended time-out is to breathe deeply while counting to ten, repeating the sequence until you begin to get a handle on yourself. If possible, remove yourself from the scene. Discharge the energy in a safe way, in a safe place: Hit a punching bag, pound a pillow, run around the block.

It is my observation that for most people, anger naturally dwindles as we come to understand the story-below-the-story. When we can see the hurt that lies below the anger, and the behavior that evoked it, the anger gradually dissolves, finally disappearing altogether. Once Trent really understood the source of Stephanie's aversion to housecleaning, he felt less personally attacked by her messiness. Once she understood the source of her aversion, she was much less likely to lash back at Trent in self-defense, accusing him of being critical and uptight.

Withdrawal

While the pattern of retreating from conflict is certainly preferable to lashing out in anger, it can be a hurtful behavior that is quite detrimental to the relationship. Walking out of the room in the midst of an argument, refusing to talk, avoiding eye contact—such behaviors can be extremely frustrating and are, in their own way, very powerful. I have found that the first step in working through such a pattern is for the person who withdraws to acknowledge how powerful the behavior is. This can be hard to do.

Sonya, the young woman who had longed for more verbal communication, told me herself, "I've always been a sulker. That's actually how I was taught, through my mother's example, to respond to conflict. I just shut down. Though I had certainly experienced the power of my mother's shutdown, I never really grasped how powerful it was for others when I did it. Maybe because when I'm shut down, I'm truly shut down—to myself, along with everyone else. The experience I have, internally, is that I'm not doing anything. I'm just kind of paralyzed, on hold."

As anyone who's ever been on the receiving end knows, withdrawal is not "not doing anything." It's a powerful defensive response that leaves the other person feeling shut out, frustrated, abandoned, and unable to get a grasp of the situation. Paradoxical as it may seem—given that the behaviors appear so different—changing a pattern of withdrawal involves some of the same techniques used to control rage. Remember that for human beings "fight" and "flight" are the twin strategies of our primal pattern of self-defense. So rather than immediately give in to the impulse to flee or shut down, give yourself a pause, breathe deeply, and count to ten. Repeat to yourself, "I can stay here. I can make eye contact. I can at least let my partner know that I won't be in this state forever."

When I last saw Sonya, she told me, "My pattern of withdrawal is so long-standing and seems to go so deep that so far I haven't been able to reverse it. It seems to be a powerful instinctive way of protecting myself—but also of protecting others. Over the years, it's kept me from saying the terrible things that were going through my mind, so I have to value it. But what I've been practicing lately is letting my partner know, 'I'm sorry, but I'm shutting down now.' That seems to be the most I can do in the immediate aftermath of an argument. Then I have to withdraw. It seems I need to put a night's sleep between me and the feelings. Then, when I wake up the next morning, we can talk about it."

For Sonya and her partner, this change—small as it may seem—has been a huge step forward. It has helped her partner have more trust when she seems to desert him. He has a better understanding of her need to withdraw, and he feels less rejected by it. Though he wishes she could "hang in there" with him longer in the heat of an argument, he has been surprised at how much it helps him to hear her say, "I'm sorry, but I'm shutting down now." When we are changing deeply embedded patterns of behavior, we need to make small moves, take small steps, but those small moves can be powerful, indeed, and they pave the way for greater transformations.

Despair
While some people lash out or withdraw in response to conflict, others sink into despair—and often, of course, despair accompanies a fit of rage or withdrawal. One young wife, whose mother had been away for long periods of time when she was very small, had an intense fear of abandonment. Every time she and her husband had an argument, she feared that he was going to walk out and never return. This tended to make her more and more agitated whenever they had a disagreement, which in turn made him feel much more defensive. This couple turned out to be an excellent example of the power of the story-below-the-story. As she began to understand the feeling of doom that came over her every time they argued, the feeling became less overwhelming. And as he understood why she became so agitated, he learned how to reassure her. Now, for example, he is able to say to her, "I'm feeling really angry right now, but I'm not going away. I'm going to work today, but I'll be back this evening."

Taking Responsibility for Your Own
Patterns of Response

Eleanor and Morton came in to see me because they felt they had been stuck in a self-perpetuating cycle for fifty years. They were in their seventies, and Eleanor said immediately, "Longevity runs in both our families, and I do not want to live this way for another twenty years!"

Eleanor's desire for more contact tended to push Morton away, thereby intensifying her behavior. As we worked to uncover the deeper stories, it emerged that Eleanor had been adored by her father, and Morton had felt ignored and neglected by his parents and was never encouraged to succeed in life. He spent all his time and energy trying to prove himself to his parents and didn't know how to give Eleanor the attention she craved. The result was that Eleanor felt ignored and Morton felt smothered. Eleanor's resentment came out in her refusal to let her husband "win" on small details. He couldn't understand why even the smallest decision was so difficult. One of their recurrent arguments was about pies: She favored Mrs. Smith's, while he favored Marie Callender's.

Over the course of our work, Eleanor began to realize that Morton didn't have to totally dote on her for her to feel important. She could validate herself and begin to pursue her dream of becoming an artist. As Eleanor took more responsibility for her own feelings, Morton felt less need to ward her off and could devote more energy to changing his own pattern. One day Morton said, "Before, when I drove up to our house after work, I'd feel a kind of panicky, claustrophobic feeling, knowing that Eleanor was in there waiting for me. But yesterday, I sat there in the driveway for a few minutes, and I told myself, 'Eleanor is not like my mother. And I am not a little boy going into my mother's house. I'm going to get out of this car and go into the house that I share with the woman I love and who loves me and wants me to succeed.'"

When we are in the grip of a powerful emotional state, the story-below-the-story can act as a powerful touchstone, bringing us a measure of clarity, a measure of distance. At first it may take a certain effort to bring the story to mind, but gradually it becomes so integral a part of our new pattern of response that it simply arises—like a good friend who comes at just the right moment to calm you down and bring you back to what really matters.

Practical Solutions to Your Current Conflict

We've been discussing the core issues that lie below the recurrent conflict. The first thing we acknowledge is, "This is not about cookies," "This is not about a fence." But sometimes, as Freud said, "A cigar is just a cigar." Even if the real issue between Stephanie and Trent was her terror of being a desperately seductive woman like her mother, she and Trent still needed to figure out how to keep the house clean! One of the benefits of getting to the story-below-the-story is that it can free us to find a practical solution to the conflict in which we find ourselves. Rather than spinning our wheels in endless, repetitive conflict, we can put our heads together and think of what to do. The word *superficial* tends to have a negative connotation—but sometimes it's helpful that, precisely because we have done our deep work, we can attend to what's right in front of us.

Let's return to Jeremy and Clare. Jeremy now understands why it's so important to Clare to feel that her sense of boundaries is respected. Clare is now much less likely to feel devastated on those occasions when he slips up. But when she bakes cookies, she's also likely to bake an extra batch for Jeremy to share with others—and that practical solution is another reward for their hard work. Both emotional and practical solutions are important and need to be addressed.

. . .

The story-below-the-story brings profound and long-lasting relief. It allows us to look at the vulnerable and young face that lies behind the demon mask of a painful argument. Once we've had a glimpse, that face—whether of a small girl called *Ug* or of a little foster boy—remains available to us. In the heat of the moment we may temporarily lose sight of it, but in the blink of an eye it can be there again to break the spell of an argument.

The point of dropping to the story-below-the-story is neither to dwell on the past nor to escape the present. Rather it is to free ourselves from the powerful and unconscious identification with the past so that we can truly focus on the current reality with our partner. This takes discipline: Naturally we want our partner to heal our primal wound, to rewrite our story-below-the-story. But the very essence of an intimate relationship is that it evokes that wound, and stirs up that story. This paradox is precisely what can make an intimate relationship so healing. However, healing within the relationship requires that we each take responsibility for healing our own deep wound. It is through becoming conscious of that wound that we at last are able to rewrite the ancient script that keeps the wound from healing. The most our partner can do for us is to support us in the process. When clients ask me, "How can I support my partner?" I tell them:

- Above all, listen.
- Try not to react defensively.
- When you feel you have a truly significant observation to share, do so with compassion in a nonjudgmental way.

The initial phase of unhooking is the hardest, because the buildup from the past tends to be thick and highly charged. As we continue, however, the task grows lighter. Without the reservoir of hurt and resentment, it becomes possible to stay current in a relationship, and this brings a thrilling sense of being able to catch conflict as it arises, to nip it in the bud. Some couples have actually told me that they now look forward to disagreeing! What used to feel like a terrible descent into quicksand can become more like an invigorating game of tossing a ball back and forth or like an intriguing challenge to creative thinking. Even if the process never becomes exactly pleasurable, it can be appreciated as a simple and powerful technique that keeps two partners dynamically in touch with one another and with their own deepest selves.

Once you have unhooked, the next phase—*really making those changes*—is sometimes daunting. This is where it's easy to get stuck, because change, though exciting *and* scary, also takes courage, responsibility, and commitment. In the next chapter we will address some of the pitfalls and fears of change, helping you take the proper steps to creating and maintaining positive differences in your relationship.

CHAPTER 4

Risks—The Fear of Change

Change is not the greatest risk to a relationship. The greatest RISK is remaining stuck.

- Change, even if it is positive, can be stressful and scary. It can make us feel lost and thrown off course.
- Comfort can sometimes create stagnancy. Ruts are comfortable because they are familiar.
- When creating new patterns, we may feel worse before we feel better, because change is unfamiliar. Our initial discomfort does *not* mean we shouldn't change.
- Letting go of old patterns requires us to take responsibility for ourselves and our actions.
- The more fluid the roles are in a relationship, the healthier that relationship becomes.

In the first few days following my Fourth of July epiphany, I was exhilarated. I felt a bit like a character in a fairy tale who had been given the secret clue to breaking a spell. I almost couldn't wait to have my next confrontation with Lucas so that I could try out my new magic words. Now when Lucas made a dismissive remark like "Suit yourself!" I would know how to hold my ground.

But even as I knew deep down that I had gained a significant insight, as the days went by, I began to feel on edge. Our recurrent conflict was destructive, repetitive, and frozen, but still, it was familiar. Never underestimate the hold that familiar patterns and habits have on you. They can override your best intentions to change, keeping you stuck in repetitive patterns that don't work. I began to wonder, *Who would I be without my habitual tendency to allow another person's "truth" to take the place of my own perceptions?* Since the days of believing that I was ugly, I was so used to deferring to someone else for my own truth that I was insecure about changing my way of thinking, even though I desperately wanted to and knew I needed to. I wasn't sure if I'd still be me. I also wondered about who Lucas would be in the face of a woman who did not immediately surrender. What would happen to the "us" that I had known?

Fear of the Unknown

Change, even when positive, is stressful. As noted in Chapter 1, a standard list that ranks stressful life events rates experiences like getting married and having a baby as nearly as stressful as a serious illness and divorce. Even getting a new pet is high on the list! Although my new insight gave me hope and a sense of empowerment, it also threatened to jolt Lucas and me out of the rut that had provided its own kind of shelter and whose contours we both knew so well. Where would we land? At this juncture I had no guarantee that things would get better between us. I knew I had to take the next step, but I didn't know if it would lead to happiness. I only knew that I could no longer continue in the old pattern.

That last statement is a crucial one, and I have often repeated it to couples. At first it doesn't bring much comfort or reassurance: It is bleak, minimal, and negatively stated. Yet the understanding that we have no choice but to move on can serve as the one ray of light that shines for us, allowing us to take the next step, then the next one, into the darkness.

Initially that ray of light doesn't penetrate very far. We know that we can't go backward, but we also realize that we can't see what lies ahead. Even though I'd written down my glossary of the words and phrases that kept me hooked, even though I'd compiled my list of alternate responses, I had no idea how Lucas would react to me. Would he come up with something that was well outside the margins of my glossary? I'd been practicing my new responses in the safety of solitude, but what would happen in the heat of interaction? Would my resolve just melt? I simply could not predict what would take place. A leap of faith was required.

Disorientation

At such a juncture we're much like emigrants departing for a distant land. We know that life in the old village has become impossible. But as we board the vessel that will take us to a new life, our strongest feelings are loss and uncertainty. We'll have to learn another language and deal in an unfamiliar currency.

And indeed much as when immigrants first land on the new shore, most couples find that the initial phase of adjustment is rocky. To let go of old patterns before their replacements have had a chance to take root is frightening and confusing. One woman said, "For so long, we've had our scripts. We knew our cues, and we knew our lines by heart. Now when we hear the cues, we don't know what to say. It's like the whole rhythm of our communication has been thrown off. There are these long silences. It feels awkward."

Although some couples find it exciting to slip out of old patterns, almost as if they've gone on a trip together to an exotic place, most people experience a strange kind of embarrassment, a sense of exposure. As one husband said, "It was suddenly like this woman I've been married to for fifteen years was a stranger. I didn't know how to talk to her anymore, how to make conversation. And there she was, living with me in my kitchen, my bedroom."

Awkward silences, a strange new rhythm of conversation, a sense of exposure—these are actually the milder symptoms of disorientation. Given the initial stress of trying to change a pattern, the negativity is very often heightened. When familiar defense mechanisms are challenged, some people fall back on even more primitive ones. The partner whose pattern has been passive-aggressive may suddenly become blatantly aggressive—or give way to emotional collapse.

It's hard enough for the person who's had an epiphany to make a change, but what about the one who hasn't? As queasy as I was about putting my insights into practice, at least they were *my* insights, and I felt both inspired and energized by them. But what about Lucas? Like many other partners in his situation, he just felt confused and threatened by my determination to change the script of our interaction. He hadn't had a great moment of truth with fireworks exploding in the background. Not long after my realizations about the fence incident, we found ourselves having another version of our recurrent argument. For him, my sudden insertion of new lines in the old script (Lucas: "What's the big deal?" Sharon: "Well, actually, Lucas, it is a big deal.") seemed to come out of nowhere. Understandably he felt wary.

"Understandably." It's easy for me to say that now, but at the time I had little understanding of his reaction. I wanted him to recognize my new insight, to endorse it, absorb it, and respond in-kind. Instead he did just the opposite. Lucas was never an openly confrontational person. When he felt truly threatened, he would withdraw. When I said, "It is a big deal," he fell silent. Though this was typical of him, I hadn't prepared for it. The conversation I'd been anxiously rehearsing went nowhere in reality.

Lucas went home that afternoon still giving me the silent treatment. Having discovered that the old hook wasn't working on me, he pulled out the heavy-duty hardware: He didn't call me for three days. So there I was, wanting to speak a new language with my partner, feeling tentative and uncertain, but left all alone in my house. Had I made a terrible mistake? Had I sabotaged my relationship with this beautiful man with whom I'd shared so many dreams for the future—our house with its wraparound porch, our trips to the cabin by the river, the hot springs in the desert?

Though Lucas eventually did call me, the next few weeks were difficult. At first it seemed as though he was going out of his way to bait me with the old lines, and we were actually getting into more arguments than ever before. Yet every time I tried to respond in a new way or explain to him why I felt the need to do so, he would shut down. If he didn't bolt out the door, he'd say something that seemed completely irrelevant to me, like "You know, maybe we should break up, because we're not truly compatible. We don't even like the same kind of music." At other times he would fall back on his powerful seductive powers, luring me with his irresistible sweetness, teasing, flattery. With the future uncertain and the present unsettled, the temptation to fall back into the familiarity of our old routine nearly overpowered me at times. All I could do was look to my little beam of light: *I can't continue as we were.* Now through my own personal work as a therapist, I know that disorientation is actually a positive, constructive sign.

Fear of Being Alone

Needless to say, I felt anything but comfortable as I tried to change my patterns with Lucas. I felt not only disoriented but also painfully alone. Some very young part of me had expected to be immediately rewarded by Lucas for my insight and brave attempt to put it into practice. But actually, letting go of old defensive patterns means taking responsibility for our own feelings. It means we can no longer put our energy into blaming the other. It means we can't go on looking to the other person to heal us from our own personal wound or to release us from the pain of the relationship. It means we have to let go of the longing to be rescued.

One couple who comes to mind in this context is Oliver and Brooke. In their recurrent pattern of conflict, Oliver would withdraw from Brooke, avoiding both conversation and eye contact, staying out late in the evenings after work, and retreating to sleep in a room in his garage. Because Brooke had grown up with a fragile mother who would disappear into her bedroom for days at a time, Oliver's behavior triggered early feelings of abandonment. Reacting to her panic, Oliver would withdraw even further. The pattern would intensify, becoming so excruciating that at times it seemed as though their long marriage would break apart. It was Brooke's realization, *I can't continue in the old pattern,* that led her to seek marriage counseling. Oliver didn't wish to participate, so Brooke entered therapy on her own. Over the course of therapy, as Brooke began to understand her own story-below-the-story, she realized that she didn't have to respond with panic every time Oliver withdrew from her. Oliver was not her mother, and she was no longer a little girl. She was a grown woman who could learn to find comfort for herself: She could call a friend, go out for a run, write in her journal, talk to her therapist. As her neediness and panicky reaction to Oliver's distancing behavior subsided, so did the intensity of Oliver's behavior. Gradually Brooke got better at seeing what triggered their conflicts in the first place. Though Oliver was still not interested in participating in marriage counseling, the work that Brooke did to free herself from her own "stuckness" had a powerfully releasing effect on both of them.

Thus the implications of following that little beam of light—*I can't continue as we've been*—are extremely significant. When we disengage from an old, entrenched pattern, we do so on many different levels. First, we disengage from the pattern itself: When Lucas says, "What's the big deal?" I don't immediately acquiesce. Second, we disengage from the person we have been within that pattern: I'm not the little girl called *Ug* who abandons her own powers of perception. Third, we disengage from the person our partner has been within the pattern: If again and again I refuse to crumple every time Lucas challenges me, then he will eventually be forced to adopt new behaviors.

Is it any wonder that the first phase of changing a deeply entrenched pattern of interaction can be so disorienting?

Loss of Support

When I stopped being hooked by Lucas's words, I found myself alone in my house, in a kind of vacuum. Despite the difficulty, despite the many times I felt I might give in and return to the old ways, deep down I felt that my resolve was strengthening, not weakening. As it did, and as the weeks and months went by, a new anxiety arose. Not only did I have to face a new sort of aloneness in relation to Lucas, I also became anxious as to how the "new me" would affect other close relationships in my life. Sometimes we discover that other people close to us have been, consciously or unconsciously, reinforcing the same negative patterns we're trying so hard to break. Rather than support us, they sabotage our efforts to grow. They collude with our partner in an unhealthy way, or they attack our resolve in some other manner.

One young woman I saw was working hard to make some important changes in her marriage. She felt she needed to claim her own voice, to assert herself as she never had before. Her husband liked to come and go as he pleased, often staying out late at night without bothering to tell her of his plans. Though she had put up with this behavior for over a year, it was becoming more and more intolerable to her. She told her husband, "When you're going to come home late, please call me." Her father, who had always been controlling, overheard one such conversation. "Why are you being so hard on him? You're lucky to have him, you know." Needless to say, his questions chipped away at her self-confidence at a time when she needed it most.

Whether or not such overt sabotage occurs, the changes we make in the sphere of our most intimate relationship do ripple outward to include our children, parents, friends, and coworkers. Even when these changes are ultimately for the best, the process itself is deeply unsettling. Sometimes it feels as though there isn't an inch of steady ground on which to stand.

Fear of Success

As difficult as it may be to admit, many of us profoundly identify with being in a negative relationship. When we begin to take an actual step toward changing negative patterns, the question, "What if I *had* a good relationship?" brings up tremendous anxiety.

Why?

One reason is that a bad relationship absorbs a tremendous amount of energy. When we're obsessing about the last argument and bracing for the next, we don't have to think about the rest of our lives, answering questions like, "What do I really want to be when I grow up?" "What could I do that would channel my creativity?" "When am I going to get my financial act together?" "When am I going to start taking care of my health?"

Another reason we fear success is that when we stay in a bad relationship, we don't have to face the question, "Am I worthy of a good relationship?"

This last question was particularly relevant for one woman with whom I worked for several years. Julia had grown up in a family in which she felt valued and rewarded only for her achievements. Her mother's health was always delicate, and—though the family included several children—Julia was the one who assumed responsibility for taking care of her mother and running the household. From the time she was a young girl, she ran herself ragged getting up early to make breakfast for the family, working hard at school, and then racing home to make dinner, do her own homework, and help her siblings with theirs. Thinking she was finally escaping the drudgery of her existence, after high school Julia married a handsome, charming young man named Kevin. Though Julia was beautiful and intelligent, she couldn't believe such a "prince" could really love her. Unfortunately her prince was an infantile and narcissistic young man and a compulsive womanizer.

On the first night of their honeymoon, as Julia and Kevin were on their way to their hotel room, he flirted brazenly with a pretty girl. Julia felt crushed, but when she brought the matter up with him later, he acted incredulous. "Why are you being so hypersensitive?" he asked her. Julia said nothing, but a shadow had already fallen over their relationship, and the pattern that was evident from this very first argument continued throughout their long marriage. Year after year he stayed out late and was resentful when Julia asked him where he was and was he having an affair. When Julia confronted him, he became defensive and somehow always managed to blame her for even questioning him. One night at a party, Julia finally reached her limit when she saw her husband kiss another woman. Julia left the party and returned home alone. Shortly after, she moved out of the house with their children and began the difficult process of building a new life. Though it wasn't easy, today, eight years later, she is a beautiful and self-confident woman who finally believes in her own self-worth. For her to ask the questions, "Am I worthy of a good relationship?" and "Am I worthy to succeed at breaking old habits and being happy?" were to question the foundation of her entire being.

The fear of success is the fear of breaking out of old habits to create a healthy relationship. Even though we want a healthy and fulfilling relationship, it's scary, because it's uncharted territory where everything is unfamiliar and foreign. It's as if all the rules we lived by are now gone and we're starting over with ourselves and our lives.

The Myth of Passion

We've seen that falling in love is often closely linked to the process of being hooked—a sense of feeling out of control. Thus we fear that if we unhook, the fire of the relationship will dwindle. The relationship will become flat, boring, without drama.

Remember Cynthia and Allen from Chapter 1, the young couple who met when they were both traveling in

Rome? They had been instantly drawn together, and their natural attraction was intensified by the power and beauty of unfamiliar surroundings. They were one of the "honeymoon couples" whose conflict began immediately after they were married, in this case when Cynthia announced she was flying back to spend a month with her parents in the Midwest. When they came to see me, they had been married for seven years and were essentially having the same conflict over and over. We were able to drop fairly quickly to the deeper story for each of them and to thereby interrupt their pattern of chronic negativity.

Unfortunately, however—perhaps in part because Cynthia was so very independent—they did not seem to have the will to build a new relationship in the clearing they had made. They eventually separated, and Allen recently informed me that he has fallen in love with someone new whom he met through a friend. What struck me as he described their relationship was how different it seemed to be from his dramatic relationship with Cynthia. He kept saying to me as if it were a contradiction, "I'm really attracted to her—but it's so smooth between us." The third time he told me this, I had to laugh. I told him he reminded me of the city folk who proclaim, "Clean air smells funny!" Some of us are so accustomed to equating love with a certain kind of passionate drama that we can't recognize the real thing when it's right before our eyes. Though true love may begin with passionate intensity, a healthy relationship is characterized by the peaceful and sustained feeling of well-being it brings.

Facing the Grief

Just as we can become fixated on a certain hyped-up image of "real love," so can we become used to a certain level of conflict. An analogy can be made to the way caffeine, which is a stimulant, actually helps some people relax by masking their deeper agitation with a layer of chemically induced stimulation. In a parallel way intense anger can function as a cover for sadness and depression. In Chapter 1, we met a husband who was so compelled to be right all the time that he would nit-pick about something as minor as the meaning of a hit in baseball rather than face the deeper sorrow and disap-pointment his wife was expressing about his relationship with her son. Over the months we've worked together in therapy, the husband has gradually become less critical and less defensive. As he has become more accepting, his wife has become more capable of expressing her own feelings of anxiety and depression. Now that she doesn't have to pour all her energy into being negative about his negativity, she can look at herself and the choices she has made that have been problematic. This process has been difficult for her, but as she has begun to admit some of her own failings, she has let her husband comfort her more. This, in turn, has helped him feel more included, and thus less apt to be critical of her son. Each has begun to let go of the need to be so fiercely right, and, as a result, some genuine intimacy has bubbled up. Their rela-tionship is more balanced.

The more fluid (i.e., less rigid and changeable according to different circumstances) the roles are in a relationship, the healthier that relationship becomes. For example, a partner in a healthy relationship might say, "I'm not always the one who wants to talk about things. Sometimes my partner initiates the conversation, and sometimes I do." The most unhealthy relationships are the ones in which the same partner makes all the plans, initiates sex, and takes care of everything concerning the children (schedules, babysitters, school conferences, and so on).

The fear of being engulfed by sadness when the flames of anger die down is not unrealistic. As we've seen, the story-below-the-story is often accompanied by powerful grief from which it takes some time to recover, and it isn't simply dispelled in the moment of insight. After recognizing the face of the little girl called *Ug,* I still had months of sorrow to work through for all the years I'd spent putting myself down.

Grieving for lost opportunities, for the unfortunate choices one has made in one's life, is an inextricable part of the process of beginning to live authentically, of letting go of the habitual pattern of conflict, of seeing into the story-below-the-story and taking responsibility for healing one's own deep wounds. This grief cannot be short-circuited, and often it is made all the more intense because it is a grief not only for oneself, but also for others about whom one cares deeply. We saw this with Julia, who had remained in a painful marriage with a narcissistic, intimidating man for fifteen years and raised children with him—a man who flirted with another woman on the first night of their honeymoon! Just imagine the self-recrimination to which she subjected herself. Seeing her anguish I did my best to reassure her that the ability to see the past in such high relief is actually a symptom of increasing clarity. How much better it was to come to her senses now rather than later! It is never too late to break old habits and patterns.

The passage through regret is a critical phase for many people, and it is a place where it's very easy to get stuck in self-recrimination. Yes, it is necessary to acknowledge the bad choices we've made, but it's most important to affirm what we have learned and to celebrate our growing wisdom and maturity. Even good people can make bad choices—and sometimes for very understandable reasons. We may choose unwisely because we are trying to heal an old wound, escape an intolerable situation, or stay loyal to someone or something from the past, or simply because we are young and inexperienced. In facing the unrelenting regret, I can think of no better antidote than these words of writer Maya Angelou: "I did the best that I could with the knowledge I had available to me at the time." Amen!

The Ultimate Risk: Discovering Limitations

Ideally two partners are equally committed to looking into the root of their conflict, but, unfortunately, this is not always the case. In some instances one partner is simply too psychologically troubled or fragile to go the distance. As a therapist it is disheartening to see someone struggling, again and again, to find release from negative patterns with a partner who is simply unwilling or unable to change.

How is it possible to gauge such inherent limitations? In my attempt to spare people the pain and waste of pouring their emotional energy into what turns out to be a black hole, I've come up with the following list of questions to help identify red flags:

- Does your partner refuse to even recognize the need for change?
- As the weeks go by, does your partner refuse to engage with you, whether by shutting down and withdrawing, by minimizing or denying that a problem exists, or by insisting that the problem is all yours?
- Does he or she verbally acknowledge that a problem exists but, despite your continued efforts, resist all change, whether by remaining passive or by actively sabotaging your overtures?

- Does your partner have a serious substance abuse problem or engage in some other form of compulsive behavior?
- Does your partner continually create some form of distraction—whether through illness, accident, threats, affairs, or some other form of emotional crisis?
- Is your partner chronically dishonest, lying about certain crucial incidents in the past, making promises that are never kept, or giving reassurances that never translate into action?
- Do you suspect that your partner may have an underlying personality disorder such as Borderline Personality Disorder or Narcissism? The signs of such serious disorders include the following:
    - Extremely rigid, controlling, and manipulative behavior
    - Excessive blaming and shaming—no matter how a confrontation starts, it always ends with you being at fault
    - An inability to apologize and take responsibility for one's own actions
    - Terror about change, which is seen as threatening and to be avoided at all costs
    - Equal fear of intimacy and of abandonment, sometimes triggering rage
    - Intense self-confidence, alternating with abysmal insecurity
    - Highly discrepant words and actions
    - Swinging between idealization and devaluation of partner
    - Rage at any attempt by partner to individuate
    - Impossibility of any equality and stability in the partnership.

An incident between Tammy and Nathan illustrates these types of limitations. Tammy was responsible and organized. Nathan knew that Tammy prided herself on this, particularly when it came to keeping to her schedule. They had made a date at the last minute, and Nathan had forgotten about it. After missing the date, Nathan deftly turned his own guilt into angry, self-righteous blame; after all, how could he be held responsible for not showing up when Tammy was so last-minute about her plans? He would not listen to Tammy and emphatically insisted that she apologize for what was his mistake. Such pseudo-logical moves may be a sign of a personality disorder and, unfortunately, can be readily accepted by a partner full of self-doubt and low self-esteem, particularly when a relationship has poor boundaries. It requires great confidence and self-awareness to resist the twisting of the truth. In this example Tammy is challenged to set her boundaries with Nathan by holding her ground, though it's very uncomfortable and unnatural to her. By doing this, however, she can move beyond Nathan's intimidating blame and change the dynamics of the relationship. It feels uncomfortable when we begin to change behavior patterns. But I always tell my clients that this is a good sign. If you feel too comfortable, probably nothing is changing!

If your partner is extremely resistant, angry, or manipulative, prone to blaming, and habitually twists your truth, you may be dealing with a person with a character disorder. In such cases the First Argument Technique may be difficult if not impossible to implement. You don't necessarily have to leave the relationship; however, the degree of intimacy you can achieve will be significantly limited.

• • •

It is only human to resist change. The fear of being alone, the fear of success, and the fear of abandonment are all well-founded elements of the process of transformation. Even the most willing and enlightened partner will feel anxious and ambivalent as deeply ingrained patterns of the relationship are shed. For most people these fears will not last forever. But if you found yourself answering yes to any of the red flag questions posed earlier in this section, and if your partner's pattern of resistance persists, then you may have to face the reality that he or she is simply not going to change. At this juncture you have two choices if you are unwilling to accept the status quo.

You may decide to focus entirely on your own transformation, trusting that your own growing wholeness will provide sufficient relief from the pain of the situation. For some people this really is enough. For example, Brooke—who used to suffer such despair whenever Oliver withdrew into one of his distant phases—feels that she has come to "a peaceful place" within her marriage. "I never got Oliver to really talk about things with me, but I finally *got* that I don't have to plunge back into a state of infantile panic every time he sulks," she said. "Sure, there are still times when I feel hurt by Oliver's coldness, but I'm just so much less reactive than I used to be—with the result that he snaps out of it much more quickly. And so the whole atmosphere, for both of us, is much more livable."

Alternatively, you may come to the sad conclusion that you and your partner must separate. It feels risky to cease a familiar—albeit negative—pattern of interaction. In a deeper sense, however, the ultimate risk, the gravest danger to which we can expose ourselves, is *not* facing up to an unbearable situation. Once your inner voice clearly states, *I can't go on as I have been,* who would you rather be— the person who makes an authentic attempt to change or the one who ignores the voice and simply goes on in the old routine?

An authentic attempt to change carries risk. Though the techniques for bringing about this change are simple to understand, they are not easy to put into practice for the reasons we've just explored. Once we look the risks squarely in the face, it is time to celebrate the great rewards of the hard work of healing. Before we turn to those rewards, let's look at one of the most serious threats that can occur in a committed partnership: the extramarital affair. Here, too, the return to the first argument can provide us with a remarkably direct path through hazardous territory.

CHAPTER 5

Affairs—
The Ultimate Challenge

No matter what the eventual outcome, an AFFAIR challenges both partners to look at themselves and their relationship in a radically new way.

- An affair is a serious symptom of a couple's profound underlying distress.
- An affair is never the answer to unresolved problems, but it may be a catalyst to address unresolved patterns.
- Every affair has at least two victims and potentially two victors.
- There is no one right way to deal with an affair: Some couples stay together, some couples separate. *Neither decision is a sign of weakness.*
- No two affairs are alike, so they have to be treated individually, with each person examining his or her part.

The territory was hazardous for Genevieve and Tyler, whose nine-year marriage was at the brink of collapse when they first came to therapy. Through tears of rage Genevieve told me that at a recent party an intoxicated Tyler had "made the moves" on three of her close friends, kissing them and using seductive language. One of the friends had confronted Tyler and insisted he tell Genevieve—and the news had left her reeling.

While she was relieved and grateful to learn that her friends had not "crossed the line" with Tyler, Genevieve still felt betrayed on many levels. From the beginning of their relationship, she and Tyler had been involved with a group of friends who thought of each other as "the family." Though they were reasonably high-functioning people, their time together revolved around alcohol, music, and dancing. A "free spirit" atmosphere existed among them, but Genevieve had always believed that it was fundamentally innocent. Now she wondered how deluded she'd been and for how long.

Tyler had told Genevieve that he felt terrible about his behavior and that he honestly couldn't understand it, because he loved her and didn't want to lose her. Still Genevieve felt such hurt and anger that she was convinced she had to leave the marriage. The situation was made even more complex by the fact that their circle of friends had begun to shun Tyler. Genevieve felt her heart being pulled in powerfully opposing directions: Though she was furious with Tyler, it pained her to see him being shamed and isolated. After weeks of intense soul-searching, she realized that she wanted to stay with Tyler, but they had serious emotional work to do.

The Causes and Challenges of an Affair

Though affairs are common, they are among the most difficult challenges a couple can face. I always tell my clients that, whatever the particular circumstances, an affair doesn't happen out of the blue. Rather the affair is an extreme symptom of a relationship that has been in trouble for some time. I also tell them that an affair is a powerful catalyst that can either end a relationship or take it to a greater level of intimacy. No matter what the eventual outcome, an affair challenges both partners to look at themselves and their relationship in a radically new way.

Like Genevieve, most people first react to an affair by feeling hurt, angry, and a profound sense of betrayal. These intense negative emotions make us feel we must end the relationship in order to preserve our dignity. Our culture adheres to a strong belief that it is weak, foolish, and degrading to stay with a partner who has been unfaithful. When a couple come to see me in the wake of an affair, we first struggle with several questions: "Can I stay?" "Will I ever be able to trust again?" "How long will the healing take?" "How will I know if I should leave?" Amid the flood of doubts and questions, what guidelines can we use?

Sorting Out the Conflict

The first step is to understand how the crisis happened. And once again I know of no more powerful tool than the First Argument Technique. As soon as a couple reveal to me that they are struggling because of an affair, I seize the opportunity to pop the question: "Do you remember the first argument you ever had as a couple?" Although I'm used to getting a surprised look with this question, couples struggling with an affair tend to look truly stunned. For them the affair is the only relevant issue; it's as though a fire has burned all the oxygen and left them no breath for talking about anything else.

"I know it may seem preposterous," I tell them. "But in that first argument, you will find both the root of your struggles as a couple and the seed of your affair."

True to form, Genevieve and Tyler looked dumbstruck when I asked them my question. But within moments a story emerged whose link to the current crisis could not have been clearer. Genevieve told me that their first argument happened before they were married. It centered on what Genevieve thought was inappropriate behavior on Tyler's part. While they were visiting a couple who were old friends of Tyler's, Tyler kissed the wife in what Genevieve thought was "more than a friendly way." Since the incident occurred in front of both Genevieve and the husband, Tyler dismissed Genevieve's concerns as over-reacting and accused her of not truly understanding him. At the time, Genevieve immediately backed down, tell-ing herself that maybe Tyler was right and that she was, indeed, overreacting. After all, no one else seemed the least bit surprised or upset by the incident.

Sadly, from that day on, Genevieve often felt that Tyler was inappropriately flirtatious with other women. She never spoke up, however; she just repeated to her-self the mantra that she was "making something out of nothing." Now some ten years later, the recent incident had stirred up all the feelings that had been brewing, sup-pressed and invalidated, just below the surface. Recalling that first argument, she was amazed to realize that she and Tyler were right back where they had started. This time, however, she vowed that she was not going to back down and that Tyler would have to take responsibility for his actions.

Affairs as Symptoms

An affair is a serious symptom of a couple's profound underlying distress. It signifies that their issues are no longer contained within the relationship. Typically, as in the case with Genevieve and Tyler, one person has gone outside the container to seek the excitement and com-fort that they were no longer finding within it. The initial secrecy of an affair implies that the person is not ready to end the primary relationship. It also reveals that he or she is not ready to directly confront the problems within the relationship.

Once it is revealed, an affair quickly brings the couple's conflicts to the surface. The great risk of an affair is that it makes these conflicts much more complicated. It adds an immense emotional charge, along with even more issues to the underlying conflict. And by definition it involves more people. Thus even as an affair arises from, and reveals, a couple's long unresolved difficulties, it exponentially multiplies and intensifies these difficulties.

Affairs generally occur because the primary relationship has deteriorated. Usually one partner has been more conscious of the deterioration. This person then becomes vulnerable to an attractive person outside the marriage who seems to offer all that the marriage does not.

Once it begins, an affair stirs up powerful feelings that are difficult to resist. Suddenly the balm needed to heal past hurts comes in the form of a new person, whose magic touch can dispel the layers of frustration and resentment. Yet very quickly difficulties crop up in the form of intense confusion, secrecy and lies, and the pull of competing loyalties and affections. Not surprisingly, relationships that begin as extramarital affairs do not tend to be long lasting. Despite the intensity of feeling that they generate, something is inherently flimsy about them. They are like tents propped up in a wind tunnel.

Changing partners is similar to "pulling a geographic"—moving to another place in order to escape problems that must be addressed from within. It is never the answer to a couple's unresolved problems. Change needs to occur within the primary relationship itself and within the heart and mind of each partner. Healing can begin when both partners see that the affair was really a symptom of a much deeper wound and that the partner who acted out was—in a confused and destructive way—asking for help.

Looking Within

Genevieve and Tyler ultimately discovered that they had been neglecting each other. From the beginning of their relationship, they had been so focused on "the family" of their friends that they had never established a sense of being family to one another. When given the choice, they would rarely opt to do something together, just the two of them. Rather they would participate as a couple in the "family," or each would go out separately with a smaller group of friends. Over the years this pattern had eroded the sense of intimacy between them. They didn't have frequent arguments, but they more or less took each other for granted. Frequent alcohol use only reinforced the lack of true vitality in the relationship.

When they pieced together the pattern, Genevieve and Tyler had an astonishing sense of revelation. Needless to say, the great a-ha! moment didn't happen for them overnight. They undertook months and months of extremely difficult work. Before they could even begin that work, however, they had to address the greatest stumbling block for most couples: blame.

Apart from those rare (and in my experience usually unsuccessful) couples who explicitly practice an "open relationship," most couples come together with an expectation of mutual fidelity. Thus in most cases an affair represents one partner's violation of the couple's fundamental commitment to one another. This violation creates an extremely polarized situation in which one person is the "wrongdoer" and the other, the "injured." How is it possible to move from this context to a mutual exploration of what led to the affair in the first place? And how is it possible to rebuild the trust that is so necessary to a healthy relationship?

The Time Frame

The first answer to both questions is, slowly! The blunt truth is that recovery from an affair is a long and arduous process. Though it takes only one act to destroy trust, it takes many acts to rebuild it. If both partners are sincerely working on the relationship, glimmers of hope will spring up all along. For most people, however, it seems to take at least a year to move through the full cycle of renewal. I've observed that the cycle follows a fairly predictable pattern. Understanding this pattern can make it somewhat easier to hang in there through the long and inevitably turbulent passage.

One young couple, Paige and Trevor, came to see me because during the past year Paige had compulsively become involved with men over the Internet. Though the relationships were "virtual," their psychic intensity left Trevor feeling as betrayed and abandoned as if they had been physically intimate affairs. Her dishonesty and secrecy about her behavior compounded his feelings of hurt and anger. In their first session it was clear to me that Paige had no idea of the extent of the damage she had done. Given that she'd confessed to Trevor and promised to mend her ways, she seemed to think that I could give them a simple formula for getting their marriage back to shipshape. Much to her dismay I told her that, though repair was definitely possible, it would not be simple. Despite their disappointment they both recognized the value of having a realistic time frame.

The Welter of Feelings
One of the reasons for the long recovery process is that an affair brings up so many complex feelings—for both partners. In the immediate aftermath of an affair, it is common for the unfaithful person to feel acute remorse,

guilt, shame, and fear. The primary relationship is no longer the gray backdrop to the exciting, secret adventure of the affair. Rather it moves into the foreground, and there it can no longer be taken for granted. It has been dealt a serious blow, and suddenly the unfaithful partner realizes that what was precious about it could be lost forever. "I had no idea this would hurt you so badly!" "I can't believe I was such a fool as to risk losing you!" "I'll do anything if you'll take me back!" Each of these is a common refrain.

Initially the unfaithful partner may even welcome the other's wrath. Having dreaded it for so long, they may experience a cathartic release in finally meeting it full-on. However, I have found that few people are prepared for how long the anger lasts. As the months go by, the refrain changes, "What more can I do to make up for it?" "She just wants to punish me forever." "Why can't he let it go?"

The feelings that arise for the "victim" of an affair are equally intense and multilayered. Even when the initial rage and hurt seem utterly justified, many people are horrified to discover such a volcano of emotions within themselves. Typically people feel entitled to erupt for a few weeks but, once the red-hot lava has spilled over, feel they should be able to return to normal.

Unfortunately the feelings don't adhere to such a tidy schedule. And though the "big picture" may be one of a slow but steady healing, from day to day and week to week bursts of anger and grief may seem to come suddenly and without warning. They are surprising and painful reminders that the trust has not yet been fully rebuilt.

Trevor, for example, was quite typical. Having accepted Paige's apology, he sincerely wanted to be able to let go and move on with their life together. When he discovered that he couldn't simply let go, he felt terribly guilty. He felt he was being a bad spouse and a bad person, incapable of the unconditional love that was his ideal.

To make matters even more complex, in the aftermath of an affair it's not uncommon for partners to experience a renewal of sexual feeling for one another. Some people worry that something is abnormal about this. To these people I say, "It's really not so surprising. After all, you're communicating intense feelings to one another, you're revealing things to one another, you've become aware of all that you have invested in this relationship. All these things can make you feel more intimate again with one another." Some people want to take the renewed sexual feeling as a sign that their relationship is all patched up and there's no more work to do. To these people I say, "Enjoy the sense of newfound intimacy between you, but remember: An affair is a sign that deep, underlying issues need to be addressed."

The Iceberg

An affair is the tip of an iceberg, the visible protrusion of something that extends deep below the surface and has been gathering over a long period of time. Once the surface of the relationship has been pierced, the layers of past hurts, frustrations, resentments, and unmet desires begin to make their presence known.

In the painful period following an affair, it is common for one or both partners to look back on the past with nostalgia and to long for the way things used to be when life was "normal." This is when, once again, I remind people that an affair doesn't come out of the blue. The pain and disconnection that made fertile ground for the affair had been building up for a long time. Now the pain is out in the open, and the old ways of covering it up are gone. This is a profoundly uncomfortable situation, but it creates a clearing in which healing and change can take place.

Sad as it is to acknowledge that the relationship has been in distress for some time, it can also bring relief. It can be empowering for the victim to realize that he or she had some serious areas of dissatisfaction even before the affair. When we are the victim in the affair, we tend to forget that we probably were unhappy as well. Once betrayed all we can think about and feel is the hurt and pain. We know we didn't want it to happen, and we feel that we'll never recover and can't believe it is happening! It is empowering, however, for the victim to take some time and remember his or her own dissatisfactions with the relationship. Maybe he or she didn't act out by having an affair, but most people in this situation can admit that they weren't happy either. This doesn't mean the affair was the right thing to do, but it does give the victim some power in the situation and a new way to look at things. And it can be consoling to the unfaithful partner to realize that he or she does not bear the entire responsibility for what went wrong.

It Takes Two

Even an affair that seems starkly one-sided isn't. It always takes two to dance the dance of a relationship and to create unresolved issues. Though to some people this may sound almost blasphemous, the truth is every affair has two victims. A victim is one who has borne the brunt of an injury, and it is accurate to say that both partners bear injuries—in the form of unresolved issues from childhood and from the current relationship. Now that all the issues are coming out in the open, the couple have a chance to stop the victim cycle, and each person can begin to take responsibility for his or her own wounds.

Once the couple start to delve below the surface, they can begin to see their own parts in the dance. Once Genevieve and Tyler emerged from the crisis of betrayal, they began to look for the deeper roots of the rift between them. Though Tyler was the one who had overtly damaged their relationship, over time Genevieve began to understand her own contribution. She saw that in their first argument she had established a pattern of distrusting her own intuition, suppressing her feelings, and letting Tyler get away with hurtful and inappropriate behavior.

In therapy Genevieve examined her lack of self-esteem. She had grown up with a domineering and depressed father. She always felt she had to do the right thing for him so that he wouldn't take his negative feelings out on either Genevieve or her mother. From a young age she learned to put up with behavior that she really didn't like and to act as if everything was just fine—exactly the behavior that she repeated with Tyler.

Gradually Genevieve realized she wasn't as laid-back and accepting as she had always tried to appear; she had a reservoir of strong feelings within her. As the therapy progressed, she began to express herself more openly, even though she often felt afraid of confronting Tyler and afraid of the new parts of herself that were being exposed. It came as a great relief to Genevieve to discover that rather than drive the two of them apart, her open communication actually brought them closer together.

In the meantime Tyler examined his own feelings of low self-esteem. Tyler had moved from the Midwest to California when he was thirteen, a crucial time in an adolescent's formation of self-image. He had found it hard to make friends and never really connected with his peers at his new school. This painful experience solidified a feeling of insecurity for him and left him yearning to be popular, the focus of affectionate attention.

At a certain point in his young adulthood, Tyler discovered that he could be quite funny and charming, and that he could use these qualities to attract the attention for which he longed. As he grew more confident, he turned into an accomplished flirt—a role he maintained long after getting married. Though his flirtations never crossed the line into actual sexual intimacy, they nonetheless represented an exit from the marriage. A continuous flow of energy was moving away from the primary relationship and into his interactions with other women.

As with Paige—the wife who had virtual intimate encounters—it took some time for Tyler to grasp that his flirtatious behavior really was a betrayal of both Genevieve and their marriage. One of the things that helped him see this was Genevieve's willingness to examine her own behavior as a part of the breakdown of their marriage. If she had remained locked in a polarized, one-sided attitude of blame, he might never have been able to grasp what it was that had hurt her so badly.

Through therapy Genevieve and Tyler discovered the root of their current crisis. Going back to the story-below-the-story—to Genevieve's difficult father and Tyler's years of loneliness—they could see the wound around which each of them had built a personality. They could see how their devotion to the "family" had distracted them and how alcohol had helped them numb themselves to their deeper pain, making it easier to push their negative feelings and difficult issues out of sight. Tyler's flirtatious behavior finally catalyzed a crisis that became an opportunity for them to examine themselves, their relationship, and their lives. They have since built a new and very strong foundation for their marriage— a marriage in which they look to one another— not to "family"—to meet their primary needs for attention, affection, and understanding.

The Power of Resilience

What makes it possible for some marriages to not only survive but actually grow in the wake of an affair? The couples who make it through are determined to look at themselves and not just cast blame on one partner, recognizing that the affair arose as a symptom of long-standing problems between the two of them. With a strong desire to make their relationship work, they understand that the work will not be quick and easy, and they adopt a realistic time frame. Deep down they know they have a genuine love for one another.

Vanessa and Jack were one such couple. Vanessa first came to me for therapy because she had been having an affair. She didn't want to leave her marriage, and she wanted to understand her conflicting feelings. We worked on a number of her fundamental issues: low self-esteem; a history of abuse in her family of origin, and an ongoing perfectionist tendency that made her feel overly responsible, anxious, and trapped. Some of these feelings were soothed while she was having her affair. However, she loved her husband, Jack, and wanted to have a family with him. After a few weeks of individual therapy, Vanessa brought Jack into the sessions. We discovered that he wanted to stay married to Vanessa, but that—understandably—he felt hurt, betrayed, and angry. Jack is a "nice guy," having grown up in a family that avoids conflict at all costs. He has trouble saying no to those he loves—especially Vanessa—and so he tends to compromise too much at his own expense. He finds it painful to think about conflict or to risk disappointing his wife.

In my first session with the two of them, we looked at their first argument, which had involved a change of location. Jack worked in a big city, but Vanessa could not imagine raising a family there. She insisted that they move to a rural setting two hours north of his job, because she felt it was better to raise a family out in the country. This required them to spend days and nights apart, as the commute was just too long for Jack to make every day with his demanding schedule. Since neither Vanessa nor Jack was very good at showing anger or dealing with conflict, they had never resolved their feelings about this move. Jack had been upset that Vanessa wouldn't be flexible about where they lived, and Vanessa had been upset that Jack hadn't really wanted to take her feelings into account. Vanessa's resentment and underlying anger contributed to her having an affair "just to feel heard and complimented again."

After a year of therapy, Vanessa and Jack resolved their underlying issues and rediscovered their deep love for one another. They were able to create a harmonious environment, and they had two children. However, five years ago they were back in therapy—and this time it was Jack who had an affair. He explained that being away from the family a lot made him lonely. He felt isolated and unhappy and unable to express his feelings to Vanessa. One thing led to another, and he was drawn into an affair with a friend.

In spite of the sense of déjà vu and the terrible feeling of betrayal, Vanessa and Jack wanted to work things out and stay together. Their commitment to one another and their devotion to their children gave them the impetus to reexamine their issues and to discover what had once again gone wrong. They saw that they had lost their ability to communicate and had fallen back into old patterns of anger and resentment. Since it was still not easy for either of them to express anger, a lot of it went underground. Like many other couples, they got caught up in the business of daily life and forgot to take care of their relationship.

We went back to their first argument and the seeds of conflict about each of them not feeling heard and appreciated. Once again, returning to the story-below-the-story helped them to recover their affection for one another. They have had to work hard to learn how to recognize and effectively express their negative feelings rather than sweep them under the rug. Many couples are not as determined and clear that they want to save their marriage after an affair. Vanessa and Jack are an example of a resilient couple who, despite some significant set-backs, have managed to stay together. In these periods of crisis, they came immediately for help with the desire to save their relationship. In so doing they have actually strengthened their marriage through this turmoil.

Vanessa and Jack have always been open to looking honestly within themselves with little resistance or defensiveness. They have taken responsibility for their actions and strive to change their old, dysfunctional patterns. These changes did not happen overnight, but there has been slow, steady progress through the years. Reflecting upon their first argument helped them to see their own individual issues. This ability, along with a great commitment to change and a deep love for one another, has enabled their relationship to grow stronger.

When It's Time to Let Go

When couples don't stay together, it has less to do with the particular circumstances of the affair than with the couple's long-term history and their willingness and ability to explore it. Sometimes it seems that the reservoir of resentment and hostility is just too overwhelming and that so much damage has been done that there is little left to salvage.

Julia and Kevin are one such couple. As described in Chapter 4, Julia accepted Kevin's assessment of her as overly sensitive when he flirted with another woman on their honeymoon. This pattern continued for the duration of their marriage. Finally, after years of enduring Kevin's uncaring behavior—his public flirtations, his habit of coming home late at night, his absence from family life—Julia came into therapy. Kevin refused. It is not uncommon for one partner not to seek help; however, therapy can still be valuable for the other partner.

In therapy Julia learned about herself and the root of her low self-esteem. As she began to get stronger, she was able to stand up to Kevin when he would tell her she was too sensitive or making a big deal out of nothing. As she began to believe in herself, she began to confront him more often. She had her own truth and believed less and less in Kevin's version. She began to see through his intimidating tactics, and, rather than accepting them or taking them on, she challenged his accusations. Kevin did not like being challenged and began to act out even more blatantly. Because Julia had gained strength in exploring her own childhood wounds, she knew as time went on that she would rather live without Kevin than live with him and be miserable.

Because Kevin was unwilling to look at himself or even to see that he might have a problem, Julia had little hope that he would change. That's why when he acted out at a friend's party, Julia finally reached her limit and decided to leave her marriage.

When one partner cannot or will not do anything to change damaging behavior, the only solution may be for the other partner to leave. To remain in a relationship in which one continues to be hurt reflects a belief that one deserves no better. It is not a failure or a sign of weakness to leave a destructive relationship. Rather it is a sign of success and strength in oneself—a sign of heightened self-esteem.

Focus on the Process, Not the Outcome

Although I work hard to help couples stay together, and I feel gratified when we are successful, I am focused primarily on the process rather than the outcome of our work together. What matters most to me is that partners be honest with themselves and with each other. Since Kevin refused to look at the part he played in the problem, Julia could not trust that he was going to change, and the marriage did not survive. Though this was sad for them and their children, I felt able to assure Julia that she had made the right decision. I told her that she had gained many tools to help her understand herself—tools that she would now be able to pass on to her children to help spare them pain in their future relationships. I told her that all her hard work of self-exploration would help her in the years of co-parenting that lay ahead for her and Kevin. Since she now understood the root of her own vulnerabilities, she would be much less likely to get hooked back into their old conflicts, and this would make life easier for both her and for her children. Finally, I assured her that when she was ready to open her heart to someone new, she now had an excellent chance of forging a healthy relationship.

Through Julia's courageous example, we can see how the process of going back to the first argument and revealing the story-below-the-story can bring great rewards even under the most difficult circumstances. In the next chapter, we have the happy task of looking more closely at these rewards.

CHAPTER 6

Rewards—
The Freedom to Love

Clearing the past brings great REWARDS. Leaving our old baggage behind, we can be fully present in the moment. Then, when conflict arises, it is only about the current issue.

- The story-below-the-story offers us a wealth of knowledge about the past and present.
- The story-below-the-story eases tension about the current conflict in a relationship and validates the deeper issues at stake.
- Knowing your own and your partner's story-below-the-story creates more tenderness, understanding, and intimacy.
- When you learn to deal effectively with conflict in your most intimate relationship, the benefits will spread to other close relationships.

While the couples we met in the last chapter were struggling over the major upheaval of infidelity, Clare and Jeremy—a couple we met in Chapter 3— were fighting over cookies. Where we last left them, they had each been able to detach a bit from the intensity of their ongoing struggle and drop below the surface issue (Clare: "You didn't listen to me when I told you not to take all those cookies!" Jeremy: "How could you be so upset about cookies?") to the story-below-the-story. Jeremy had made the link between his desire to share the cookies with his coworkers and his early life as a foster child who never had enough of anything to share. Clare had made the link between her extreme frustration at Jeremy's behavior and her past as a girl who felt no one ever listened to her.

In this chapter we will explore the many rewards for learning about your story-below-the-story. By using this tool instead of what we usually use in arguments—shaming, blaming, and self-righteousness—we can change the patterns of our arguments, our relationships, and ourselves. This chapter will demonstrate how the story-below-the-story creates more empathy, validation, and clarity in our relationships. It will show how taking responsibility for ourselves, clearing away the past patterns, and learning to stay current in our relationships create a strong foundation for making all of our relationships healthier and happier. The rewards of the First Argument Technique create a ripple effect in your life and can be used with any relationship, including intimate relationships and those with siblings, friends, coworkers, and others. Our story-below-the-story is a tool that, when used correctly and consistently, brings fulfillment in our relationships, with the opportunity to build harmony and intimacy rather than discord and distance with our loved ones.

The Ability to Feel Empathy

For Clare and Jeremy, as for most couples with whom I've worked, the first reward of dropping to the story-below-the-story is self-forgiveness. Often when we're locked in repetitive conflict, we're not aware of the extent of self-condemnation involved until it diminishes. Now that Clare understood the source of her seemingly disproportionate anger, she no longer felt like an irrational shrew. Now that Jeremy understood why he had ignored Clare's request, he no longer felt so guilty and defensive. Almost immediately the atmosphere between and around them was altered, much as if a dark, heavy cloud was suddenly suffused with light. When neither partner is oppressed with feelings of self-doubt and self-condemnation, the situation is already greatly alleviated. Instead of each partner being poised to protect the old wound and fend off an attack from the other, tenderness arises. For the first time Clare could feel a genuine empathy for her own childhood self, and Jeremy for his.

Quite naturally this tenderness spread between them. Now when Clare looked at Jeremy, she could see the little foster boy inside the "inconsiderate husband." When Jeremy looked at Clare, he could see the unheard, unseen girl inside the "controlling wife." This reaction serves as a pivotal moment in the process of healing, and it can provide a touchstone throughout a couple's future interactions. Whenever tensions begin to run high, and the couple faces imminent danger of being hooked by an old pattern, they can now tap back into the tenderness that spontaneously accompanied the first move to the story-below-the-story.

Finding Validation

The wonderful thing about this process is that, while easing tension around the current issue and helping both partners recover empathy for themselves and for each other, it validates the real issues at stake in the conflict. For me as a therapist, this is a significant benefit, because when people first come in for counseling, they're often afraid that their concerns are going to be dismissed and that they themselves are going to be seen as petty, unreasonable, and immature. This was certainly the case with Jeremy and Clare, who initially confessed that they were "arguing over the stupidest things." Once we had discovered the story-below-the-story, they no longer had to spin their wheels over a batch of cookies—but they didn't have to dismiss the cookies as trivial or meaningless, either. The same was true for me in my argument with Lucas over the fence. I didn't have to keep arguing with him about it, but when he said, "What's the big deal?", I could say, with confidence and without embarrassment or apology, "Well, actually, it is a big deal for me."

The fence was a big deal for me because, as I came to see, it was linked to the deeper issue of our relationship: my profound self-doubt and how it hooked into Lucas's need to feel he was in control and always the cool, self-confident guy.

The Relief of Clarity

When we discover and clarify what's been at stake in our ongoing conflicts, we feel a sense of validation. After revealing our story-below-the-story, it suddenly makes sense why we could never resolve the "silly" fights. Understanding now that the arguments weren't about silly things after all, we realize we're not crazy for the feelings we were experiencing. For me, as for Clare and Jeremy, and so many of the couples with whom I've worked, such clarity brings a powerful sense of relief. It is a relief to know that there is hope for change, rather than feeling stuck in the same repetitive patterns that led to nowhere. Without clarity we travel in a million different directions trying to solve the wrong problem. Once each person gets clear about his or her own issues, there is a sense of relief: "At least I know what we're really arguing about now, and at least I have a direction for resolution." When we can identify the underlying issue and acknowledge that issue without guilt and apology, without defensive maneuvering and reactive behavior, it's as though someone has beamed a ray of light on a capsized boat in the night sea. Rather than feeling submerged, thrashing about in darkness and confusion, now we can see where we are. We can see in which direction to swim.

When I first set eyes on Haley and Cody, they were sitting stiffly at opposite ends of my couch. Not long into their session, they told me that they were both feeling great despair about the ever-growing disconnection between them. They seemed to have less and less to say to each other, and it had been months since they had been physically intimate. Neither seemed able, looking at the present context, to offer any sort of explanation. But when I asked them if they remembered what their first argument had been, Haley found her voice. "I couldn't possibly forget it," she said, "because it happened at such a crucial moment. It wasn't really an argument, but it was the first big crack that came between us. It was the first time we spent the night together, and Cody said something to me about the way I was making love with him. I never really recovered from that. From the beginning of our relationship, I'd been afraid that he would compare me with his first wife, whom he'd always described as really beautiful and seductive. That first experience just confirmed my fears. For a while after that, I was able to just sort of be there physically with him, while pulling away emotionally. But gradually, I couldn't even do that anymore. I just felt too vulnerable."

When Haley stopped talking, we sat in a long silence. Cody looked stunned. Finally, in words that were as halting as Haley's had been fluent, he told her how terrible he felt that what he remembered as "one of those stupid, random things that just pops out" could have hurt her so badly. Looking straight into her eyes, he told her, "What you've never really understood is how afraid I was of losing you." Having been left by his first wife for another man, he had been overwhelmed by the intensity of his feelings for Haley. "That's what my stupid little remark was about," he said. "I just couldn't let you see how much I cared." As I watched the two of them weep with relief, it was hard to believe they were the same couple that had been sitting so stiffly in their separate worlds just moments ago. It hadn't even taken much probing on my part to yield the story-below-the-story that made it possible for them to truly see each other through the fog of hurt and disappointment.

Taking Responsibility

When we drop to the story-below-the-story, we gain a wealth of self-knowledge in condensed form. With this knowledge comes responsibility. Once I recover the little girl standing before the mirror, it becomes my responsibility to remind her that she's not the ugly creature she thinks she is. It's up to me to keep from plunging back into self-doubt when my partner challenges me, belittling my concerns and implying that I'm overly emotional. It's my task to stay focused the next time an argument arises— whether over a fence, a wraparound deck, or planting grass seed. I must make the effort to not get swept into the surface turbulence, but to remember the deeper issues that are at stake.

With each of these moves, I embody the true meaning of responsibility, which is formed from the words *response* and *ability*. I feel a need, a lack, a hurt—and I respond, out of my own strength, out of my own knowledge of my self, and from what I have learned about my story-below-the-story. I now have the ability to communicate differently to my partner about my feelings. This is the exact opposite of placing blame outside of myself, which, as we've seen, is a common defensive pattern. If my partner is also taking responsibility for himself, we can shortcut or even avoid an argument. We can talk about our own issues and what we're feeling. We both can be responsible for ourselves, thereby changing the entire dynamic of the relationship. Just imagine a relationship where disagreements could actually bring you closer together!

We might be tempted to think that this way of approaching conflict—taking responsibility for our own actions and words is rather harsh and self-depriving, but it's actually quite the opposite. It's not like the Little Red Hen who has to do everything herself because everyone around her is so unreliable. Rather this new "I'll do it myself!" arises from compassion for oneself and the desire to change old patterns within yourself that you know don't work for you. It is a more empowering feeling to change what doesn't work within yourself than to constantly blame your partner for your unhappiness. Time after time I have seen the satisfaction that people get when they've had the courage and strength to change an old pattern. An interesting phenomenon occurs. Once we have taken responsibility for our own life and changes, suddenly the actions or inactions of our partner don't seem quite as important. To shift from blaming to taking responsibility is the beginning of a whole new way of looking at life. We now have the freedom and knowledge to change the dynamics of our relationship with ourselves and with others.

Only when I allowed myself to truly feel the sadness of the little girl called *Ug* could I take responsibility for my role in the ongoing drama with Lucas. A similar shift happened in the life of Stephanie, the young woman whose mother cleaned the house only for her boyfriend.

Not until Stephanie could feel compassion for her girl-hood self could she let go of her current resistance to housecleaning, along with the shame and anger that were bound up with that resistance and damaging her relationship with Trent.

Through these examples we can see that taking responsibility for oneself is difficult and involves letting go of some old, ingrained, and self-indulgent patterns; yet it is actually a great reward. It is the natural fruit of coming to see more clearly and developing more com-passion for oneself. As we become responsible for our-selves, self-confidence blossoms. When we're not seeing another person as the source of our difficulties, as the obstacle to our happiness, we are free to create that happiness for ourselves.

One of my clients, Deirdre, was always complain-ing about her husband's domineering presence. Though they had a very traditional marriage, in which he was the breadwinner and she was the homemaker, Deirdre had carved out only a tiny space for herself in the house. In our first few sessions together, her complaints kept esca-lating: "He has taken over the entire house!" "He's tak-ing over the garage!" "Now I have to park on the street because the garage is full of his cars!" One day, just as I was on the brink of confronting Deirdre about her own part in the pattern, she suddenly stopped herself in the middle of one of her rants. "Wait a minute!" she exclaimed. "What's my part in all this?" In the weeks that followed, Deirdre was able to see why she had allowed her husband to take over all the space. She saw that as long as she was busy bumping into his massive clutter, she didn't have to take the risk of actualizing her own desires. She'd always dreamed of writing, but how could she? There was no space for her! When she stopped put-ting all her energy into blaming her husband, she could muster some compassion for herself and face the anxiety that was keeping her from living her own life.

Clearing the Past

When we uncover the story-below-the-story, we invite a lost part of ourselves into awareness and offer compassion to that hurt child. In this way, as we've seen, we heal the pain of the past by opening our hearts and taking in that lost child and understanding his or her pain.

One of the great mysteries of the human psyche is that it's not until we fully let the pain in that we can let it go. And letting go is yet another great reward of this process. To give just one of many possible examples: Daniel and Alisa were a young couple who came to see me in order to facilitate the process of dissolving their marriage. During their first session, Alisa explained that while she had been pregnant with their now one-year-old daughter, Daniel had had an affair. Needless to say the timing was devastating to Alisa. Just when she had felt that powerful pull inward to the circle of their growing family, he had broken that intimacy by turning to someone else. Just when she had felt a special need for his support, he had been unavailable to her. When the baby was born, she had felt, "Daniel wasn't there for me during the pregnancy. This is *my* child."

By the time they came to see me, Daniel had certainly realized how much he'd hurt Alisa. He felt that he'd done his utmost to apologize, but he said, "Alisa won't stop punishing me." It was as though he was no longer entitled to have any say whatsoever about their family life. He felt that Alisa had become domineering, and what hurt him most was that he felt excluded from a relationship with their daughter. "I just can't get in," he kept repeating.

Though initially they were determined to break up, over the course of therapy Daniel and Alisa decided to stay together. The turning point came when they realized that long before Daniel had the affair, they had essentially been having the same argument over and over again. When they first met, Daniel was only eighteen years old. Besides being a few years older than Daniel, Alisa had a more demanding job and earned more money. When they bought a house together, it was under Alisa's name. From the beginning their recurrent conflict centered on Alisa's belief that Daniel was "irresponsible." Her own father had always been an untrustworthy man, and it was easy for her to assume that Daniel was similar—though, in fact, he was not. He was just young. In therapy Alisa realized that she had used Daniel's affair as the ultimate validation of her lack of trust in Daniel—but, in fact, she had never trusted him. Because of her painful history with her father, she had never felt able to trust any man.

As for Daniel, he came from a family with an overpowering mother and an absent father, so he never trusted his own intuition and inner strength. He had learned to give in up to a certain point, after which he tended to get angry and leave. In therapy Daniel realized that this pattern was destructive both to himself and to their relationship.

As they sifted through their memories, Alisa came to feel that the greatest obstacle between them was not really anything Daniel was doing in the present. Rather it was her own inability to let go of the past. It was a question not of forgetting the hurt or the anger she had felt over Daniel's affair, but of no longer allowing those emotions to hold the central place in her marriage. She realized that she had to let go of the affair as a kind of touchstone, a reference point that justified her ongoing punishment of Daniel. When she did, it finally created an opening for him. And since he had broken his old pattern, he was finally able to step into the family circle, participate in decisions, take on more responsibility—as well as make more demands of her. "That's my child, too!" he told her.

Though the initial adjustment was difficult, Daniel and Alisa were both immensely relieved by the closeness and balance they recovered. They began to experience a greater degree of intimacy than they ever had before. Now that Alisa had seen into the deeper roots of her distrust of Daniel, she felt able to see him without the layers of projection from her own childhood. No longer living with the constant accusation that he was "irresponsible," Daniel finally began to blossom as Alisa's full and equal partner in the marriage.

Early on in every relationship, patterns develop. A pattern is simply a series of events that becomes predictable over time. She pays the bills, he does the gardening. He's the first to notice when communication has broken down, she's the first to notice when the house is messy. Whatever the established pattern, it continues to automatically repeat itself in the relationship until it either doesn't work, or we get tired of repeating the same thing over and over again, with no resolution. Patterns are very strong and have a life of their own, unless they are examined and changed. After a while they are so predictable that we can see where an argument is going before we've barely said two words to our partner.

Many people with whom I've worked have been amazed to discover that as they let go of certain patterns within their current relationship, they are simultaneously released from the same patterns within a relationship that has already ended. One of my clients was rereading her old journals when she made a connection between her ex-husband and her current partner. Though they appeared to not have many similarities, she realized "what they had in common was me." Both were also domineering men. Her current partner was domineering in an overt way: He had a loud voice and an assertive, self-confident manner and insisted on controlling their day-to-day plans. While her ex-husband had been a soft-spoken man, he had steadfastly resisted her intense desire to have a child. Now, for the first time, she was able to see how in both relationships she had permitted her partner's needs and desires to overwhelm her own. In taking a step forward in her current relationship, she also had a powerful feeling of letting go of the role that had oppressed her years ago.

Forming New Patterns

As we clear the past, as we continue to put our new insights into practice, we find that we become much less reactive. We're no longer so easily hooked back into the same old grooves, so easily swept up into surface issues. Growing freer of defensiveness, of the patterns of blaming and shaming, we create a clearing in which we can learn new patterns of interaction.

Thomas and Steven, another couple with whom I worked, are a powerful example of such transformation. From the beginning I felt a deep core of affection between them, but the dynamic was clearly out of balance. Steven is nurturing and demonstrative by temperament and Thomas is quite reserved. While both had demanding jobs, Steven did most of the domestic work of cooking, cleaning, and maintaining the house. By the time they came to see me, Steven was feeling overworked and underappreciated, while Thomas was feeling constrained and controlled. The more Steven seemed to crave affection, the more Thomas withdrew. They had stopped being physically intimate with one another, and both felt themselves inside a spiral that was spinning them farther and farther apart.

After some weeks of meeting with me as a couple, Thomas came to see me individually. He told me that he had begun to feel that there was something in his pattern of withdrawal that had nothing at all to do with Steven. Over the next few months, he unearthed an early experience of sexual abuse. Needless to say, the process of unearthing took great courage—much more than it had taken to simply react to Steven. Gradually, as he was no longer putting his energy into resisting Steven's affection and generosity, he could begin to take some of it in. Having discovered his own story-below-the-story, he could appreciate that Steven really was the right person to help him heal.

Both Thomas and Steven worked hard at changing their patterns, and their relationship is now much more balanced. Their story illustrates that one of the great rewards of this process, the First Argument Technique, is that it can bring us full circle to appreciate the positive aspects of what attracted us to our partner in the first place, when we fell in love. There had been little love in Thomas's family, and in Steven he had found a truly loving man. It's not surprising that he wasn't immediately able to open to Steven's love—but when he did, he knew he'd found exactly the medicine he needed.

Staying Current

When we clear the past, when we make a space in the present for new patterns of interaction, we receive the wonderful benefit of staying current in our relationships. As the reservoir of resentment decreases, we begin to reap the results of our work. Issues come up, but they carry significantly less charge. Before an argument seizes us, we can feel it coming, and we can notice the trigger before we press down on it.

One couple, Naomi and Karl, had nearly broken up several times over an issue that had been with them from the beginning of their relationship. Although Karl was devoted to Naomi and had never been unfaithful to her, he ardently believed in the doctrine of "nonpossessive love." For quite a few years before meeting Naomi, he had openly practiced this doctrine and had had a number of overlapping relationships, which, he insisted "everyone involved was fine with." In the early years of their relationship, Naomi was insecure about this aspect of Karl and his past. "I wanted him to come out and renounce it to me in some way, to declare that he had changed his ways. The more I pushed, the more he would dig in his heels, and we would go around and around. More than once he told me I seemed to be goading him to go out and find somebody else, and several times it really looked like we were going to split up."

As with the other couples we've seen, what changed the situation for Naomi and Karl was that they came to understand the deeper story. By applying the First Argument Technique, they uncovered that since she was abandoned by a severely depressed parent when she was a tiny girl, Naomi had an especially strong need to be reassured of her partner's devoted presence. Having been raised in a rigid, fundamentalist Christian family, Karl couldn't bear to feel that his freedom was being constrained by someone else's beliefs. As Naomi put it: "Now when his polyamorous shtick comes up, it's like we can both see the gears spinning, but we don't engage. We just don't have to do that anymore. Sometimes we can even laugh."

A major discouraging factor that couples face is the feeling that there is so much baggage, so many issues, so many fights, that they don't know where to begin or how to solve them. It feels bleak and overwhelming. Therefore one of the key goals I have as a therapist is to clear away the past and bring the couple into the present, where they now know that each argument they have is connected to their core issues. This is accomplished with the First Argument Technique. As we saw with Karl and Naomi, once they discovered their story-below-the-story and were aware of when and how their core issues got triggered in an argument, they could at that point come right to the present with questions and comments such as: "How are we feeling now? What are we arguing about now? Our core issues must have just been triggered, or we wouldn't be fighting. So let's revisit our core issues and talk about that." This helps because they can focus on the deeper issues that are triggered, rather than wasting their time and causing more hurt by arguing about the content issue of the argument.

When we become current with each other (meaning there are no unresolved arguments lurking in the background), an argument is manageable and not that hard to solve. It's the build up of unresolved arguments and the continual recycling of those past arguments that overwhelm us, making us feel hopeless and helpless. When we become current in our relationship, we feel confident that we can solve this one particular problem and move on. Less and less time is spent on conflict, and more and more time is spent enjoying one another. I've seen it with so many couples, like Naomi and Karl, where they actually laugh about issues that once felt insurmountable.

The Ripple Effect

As we become more aware and responsible in our most intimate relationship, the process can extend outward, bringing relief to other close relationships. Sometimes this extension happens spontaneously, as a natural consequence or ripple effect of the work we've done with our partner. Other times, the effort is more methodical and consciously directed. What's important is to realize that with family members, friends, and even coworkers, we can use the three-step First Argument Technique of peel, reveal, and heal to release us from negative patterns of interaction.

Family Dynamics

One young woman who came to see me, Kirsten, had a complicated history with her sister, Jenna, which had recently come to a head over a young man named Aaron. Kirsten had been doing a lot of things with Aaron, a good friend she'd been spending a lot of time with for several months. Kirsten was always looking out for Jenna, and it began to weigh on Kirsten that her sister was always home alone. Within the months that Kirsten knew Aaron, however, Jenna and Aaron talked periodically, and he eventually asked Jenna out on a date. Before Jenna went out with Aaron, she cleared it with Kirsten to make sure that she felt okay about them dating. Kirsten reassured Jenna that she was happy for Jenna and felt fine about it, and Jenna and Aaron started dating. After they had been going out for awhile, Kirsten started to feel uncomfortable with the situation. As Kirsten explains it, "On the conscious level, I thought I was just sort of 'loaning' Aaron to Jenna, and they would just be friends. But then they actually became involved with each other, and it was just too much for me."

At our first session in my office, Kirsten was truly distraught about the love triangle. When we applied the First Argument Technique, dropping down to the story-below-the-story, however, she could see the dynamic that had laid the foundation for the current crisis. Though Jenna was the older of the two girls, she had learning disabilities that had made her life difficult from early childhood. She had a rather fragile personality, low self-esteem, and few friends. From the time she was quite young, Kirsten had felt that she was the strong one, responsible for taking care of Jenna. In "loaning" Aaron to Jenna, she was simply continuing a pattern that had begun years before when, as she put it, "Our parents switched our birth order and declared me the big sister."

Sitting there in my office, Kirsten remembered the moment it first happened. She was eight years old, Jenna was ten, and one day their mother knocked on Kirsten's bedroom door and told her, "When your friends come over today, I want you to be sure and include Jenna, because she doesn't have any friends." According to Kirsten, the pattern had greatly intensified in junior high. "Peer pressure is so difficult at that age. I was desperately trying to keep my own head above water, and I had this frightened older sister clinging to me, convinced that she could only have a life through me."

Now becoming fully conscious of the pattern for the first time, Kirsten realized she could choose to not repeat it. "I will always care about my sister," she told me. "But I'm not her older sister, and it's not up to me to live her life for her. I'm entitled to have a life of my own." She paused for a moment, and I will never forget her smile as it suddenly occurred to her, "I could go traveling!" In her twenty-eight years, she had never before felt that she was permitted to leave the city where she and her sister lived, for fear of abandoning Jenna. As for Jenna, she came to realize that she was stronger than anyone had given her credit for, and she felt restricted by the assumption that she could not take care of herself, when in fact she could.

As intense as the relationship between siblings can be, there are few family relationships as intense as those between parents and children—especially parents and teenage children. One family came to see me because the parents were beside themselves with anxiety, frustration, and anger with their seventeen-year-old daughter. They felt she had been acting out for years, disobeying their rules and going out with a "fast crowd." The most recent crisis had occurred when she drove her mother's car without asking permission and smashed it. Fortunately no one had been hurt. But the three of them were barely speaking to each other, and the tension during our first session was so extreme that I had one of those long moments of wanting to make a dash for the door.

Drawing a deep breath I asked the daughter, "Do you remember the first argument you and your parents had that was somewhat like this argument about the car? A time when you did something you knew you weren't supposed to do, and they found out about it?" She did. It had happened when she was twelve years old—just on the brink of adolescence—and she had told her parents that she was spending the night at one friend's house, when in fact she spent the night at the house of a girl whom her parents didn't like. When her parents found out about her deception, they were furious and hurt. Remembering this earlier argument—which now seemed minor to all of them, compared to the smashed-up car—the family was able to focus on the underlying dynamic. "It's always been about trust," the daughter said. She seemed both relieved and amazed to have had this revelation.

For the first time a situation that had seemed hopelessly blocked seemed workable. In the weeks that followed, we explored ways the parents could demonstrate more trust in her and that she could prove herself worthy of that trust.

Challenging Friendships

Friends, too, can use the same techniques of identifying the pattern, finding the hooks, dropping to the story-below-the-story, and working to create new patterns. Carmen came to see me in the wake of a major falling-out with one of her closest friends, Polly, a woman she had known since girlhood. Carmen was about to be married, and, according to her, the immediate source of her conflict with Polly was that "she's taking over my wedding plans!" The two women had known each other since kindergarten, so Carmen wasn't sure she could reconstruct their very first argument, but she was absolutely clear about the pattern. From the beginning Polly had been both envious of her and bossy. As Carmen remembered the various girlhood dramas and the jealousy that was present—birthday parties, school plays, camping trips, and double dates—she felt validated in her current distress, but she also gained a sense of perspective.

Though it was not easy, given the emotional magnitude of a wedding, Carmen was able to gain some detachment from the immediate situation. With this detachment she could create some boundaries with Polly in a firm yet compassionate way despite Polly's inability to talk openly with Carmen about their relationship. Carmen was disappointed that the process wasn't more mutual, but she gained considerable relief from her own effort to drop below the surface. Having known Polly for so long, it wasn't particularly difficult for Carmen to understand the source of Polly's envy. This understanding made her feel more compassionate toward Polly, even as it clarified her own need for self-protection. Just as with a couple, a troubled friendship can greatly benefit from the process of seeing the ongoing pattern and dropping to the story-below-the-story, even if only one person takes the initiative.

Complicated Coworker Relationships

The First Argument Technique is effective with coworkers as well. Rebecca and Serena worked together in a college setting. Rebecca was Serena's boss. They were also friends outside of work. When Rebecca and Serena were in their friend mode, they were equals, and Rebecca was actually more likely to go to Serena for advice and for sharing confidences. However, as soon as they got into work mode, Rebecca admittedly would pull rank on Serena, treating her as an underling and apparently forgetting their friendship.

Rebecca was raised in an academic family in which her father was the authority figure, and attention and affection were linked to accomplishments. When Rebecca was working, she felt she had to be perfect and run the program in an "official" way. She tended to forget her own humanness and that of her coworkers. She was dogmatic, punitive, and unyielding—the opposite of the way she was outside of work. Serena came from a family where she was often criticized by her brother, and she was just beginning to gain confidence in her intelligence and efficacy. When Rebecca would call her to task for not doing her job exactly as Rebecca expected, Serena felt humiliated and confused, especially since their friendship was so different.

Both Rebecca and Serena cared about their relationship, and therefore they discussed their problems with me. I suggested they look at their first argument and their story-below-the-story. Their first argument was actually a disappointment: When Serena had interviewed for her job, Rebecca had not wanted to hire her, perceiving Serena as too young and inexperienced. The other people on the hiring committee had disagreed, and Serena was hired, subsequently excelling in her position, at least according to others. Rebecca continued to perceive Serena as incompetent, and she often treated Serena as if she weren't doing a good job.

Once they made the connection between their current conflict and each other's story-below-the-story, Rebecca realized she was still trying to get her father's approval by being the "perfect administrator." She could then let up a little on Serena and others in the department. Even though Serena had a different work style from Rebecca, Rebecca could recognize Serena as effective in her work. Rebecca's criticism was not warranted. Serena realized that Rebecca was not her brother and that she could reason with her, express herself directly, and trust that she would listen. Through looking at their individual issues, Rebecca and Serena were able to understand one another and work more effectively together without their old issues getting in the way.

The Fluidity of Time

Perhaps the greatest reward of the First Argument Technique is the way it enables us, in a simple and economic way, to address conflict in every dimension of time. As we've seen, by recovering the story-below-the-story, we are able to address a deep wound from the past. By understanding how we get hooked, we are able to change our patterns in the present and stay current in our relationships. The approach also has a predictive quality. When the first argument arises at the beginning of a new relationship, we have the tools to assess whether this relationship is truly worthy of a future.

For example, Makela, a friend of mine who is familiar with my work, had been seeing a man named Sean for several weeks when they had their first conflict. Makela is a writer, and for over fifteen years she had established the habit of writing every morning. From eight to twelve o'clock on weekdays, she avoids appointments and social engagements, and she stays away from the phone and other distractions. Her close friends know this about Makela and respect it. But Sean could not.

"Almost from when he first met me, he made little jabs about my writing schedule, about how 'uptight' and 'inflexible' I was," Makela told me. "Then, just a few weeks into the relationship, he threw a real fit one morning when I wasn't available to go out to breakfast with him. I really liked a lot of things about Sean, and in the past I would have hung in there much longer, enduring his resentment of my work and, in some way or another, pleading with him to understand. But this time, really looking at the dynamic of that first argument, I knew that this was not the right relationship for me. My life as a writer is such an important part of me, and if someone who claims to really like me doesn't get that about me in the beginning or can't tolerate it—it just doesn't bode well. It was painful to end the relationship like that, and it seemed very abrupt to Sean. But I know I did the right thing. I felt that I spared both of us months, and perhaps even years, of having the same fruitless argument," which would have led to resentment, anger, and pain for both of us.

Some people worry that, with such a powerful tool to assess compatibility, they will be tempted to break off connections too quickly, letting go of relationships before they've really given them a chance. I reassure them that this need not be the case. What's important is to analyze that first argument and ask yourself, "Where am I at risk of getting hooked?" In Makela's case she knew that her Achilles heel was an old guilt about being more gifted and more focused than her older sister, who was a painter. This, she knew, was not a wound that she needed to reopen. She had worked hard over the years to claim her right to take herself seriously as a writer, and, in her words, "I didn't want to waste any more of my precious life energy struggling with an envious person who wasn't okay with what is one of the most important things about me."

Once you've discovered the core or root of that first argument, the next question to ask yourself is, "Is this a place that really needs to be healed in my life? Is this a place that I need to reopen, or have I already learned this lesson?" In Makela's case she knew that there were certain things that were not negotiable for her in a relationship, like dealing with an envious boyfriend. She knew that this was a core issue for her because of her sister's jealousy. She was positive that this dynamic would not work for her in a relationship, and she didn't have to relearn this fact. Therefore she was able to quickly end the relationship with her boyfriend.

Another woman I know, Payton, attended one of my seminars many years ago. She has now been happily married to her husband, Emilio, for fifteen years. She told me how she was able to use the first argument she had with him to help her recognize that Emilio was the right man for her. For Payton, her first argument with Emilio had to do with trust. As a child she watched her mother cheat on her father, and she didn't want that kind of relationship. When she spoke to Emilio about doubting his faithfulness, he was able to tell her, without getting defensive, that he also valued faithfulness. He went on to say that if he had given her any reason to distrust him, like being overly attentive to an ex-girlfriend, he would not do that anymore. He wanted to build trust with Payton, not push her away. Therefore, in this case, their first argument clarified that their values were the same, and they have since built on that to create a healthy marriage.

"Early on in our relationship," Payton said, "I noticed from our very first argument that we were having the same conflict over and over. It would come up when Emilio was feeling depressed and discouraged about his work, and instead of giving him support at that time, I would withdraw from him. Dropping to the story-below-the-story, I could see how I was getting hooked right back into a very painful pattern in my childhood. I always felt that my mother pulled away from me when I was sad—and here I was doing the same thing to Emilio. I realized that this really was a pattern from which I wanted to heal. I wanted to learn how to give comfort to someone whom I loved. And I knew that in doing so, in discovering that strength within myself, in some way I'd be comforting the little girl I used to be. In so many other ways, Emilio and I were wonderfully compatible—and my understanding of our first argument really helped me to say yes to this wonderful man."

In my own life, my relationship with Lucas did not survive the insights that came to me on that Fourth of July. We struggled on for several months until, emboldened by my new clarity, I was able to extricate myself from a chaotic and unhappy situation that, given its intensity, might have continued for a long time. Putting my new insights into practice, in the few years that followed I was able to very quickly let go of some potentially unsatisfying relationships. Though at times I did feel lonely, I was encouraged by the knowledge that I now had the tools to truly recognize the right man for me when he came. And five years after Lucas and I broke up, I did recognize the right man. I married my husband, Michael, in a friend's beautiful vineyard in the Northern California Wine Country.

• • •

The entire process of breaking the argument cycle by identifying your first argument, understanding its significance, and using that information to change old patterns, is not an easy undertaking. However, as we have seen throughout this book and especially in this chapter, there are great rewards if we work at transforming old habits that don't serve us. It can be an overwhelming process, but by breaking the task down into smaller pieces, the process becomes less discouraging and more doable. My hope is that you will be inspired and encouraged to take the plunge into change by recognizing the gift your first argument brings, identifying your hooks, and learning your story-below-the-story so that you can reap the rewards that minimize destructiveness and pain and maximize goodwill and love. As we will see in the next chapter, that's what happened for me.

CHAPTER 7

Reprise

The defense mechanisms we learned as children are the very things that threaten our adult relationships. We unknowingly repeat these patterns throughout our lives. When we examine the first argument to find these patterns and their roots, we begin the healing process and once again find hope.

- If you are willing to drop into the root of your conflict, you really can't lose. In the end, no matter what, you are going to know a great deal more about yourself.
- The remarkable thing is that the conflict we so dread can itself provide the antidote to our issues.
- The clearing we make within ourselves, the freedom we find within our own inner conflict, the ability to turn the "poison into a remedy," are the greatest gifts we give ourselves.

It was a hot summer day, and in four days I would be married. In the five years since that desperate Fourth of July, I had come a long way. I had unhooked from my relationship with Lucas and met a man who confirmed that a harmonious relationship was possible. I didn't have to be in a state of constant disequilibrium. I had found a strong and gentle man with whom conflict, when it arose, could be faced without locking into a painfully self-perpetuating pattern.

In the frantic last days before the wedding, I was living on take-out food, and on this particular day I was leaving the local Chinese restaurant with my dinner in a bag. Eyes straight ahead, engrossed in the thousand and one things I still had to do, I was heading for the door when a grinning face diverted my attention. At first I didn't recognize that face. It had no place in my new world. But then I saw that it was Lucas, with whom I hadn't crossed paths in two years. I couldn't help but smile back and reflect on the impeccable timing. Just as I stood on the brink of a new life, here was a chance to recognize, face-to-face, that I had truly let go of the past.

Lucas and I exchanged the usual pleasantries: "Hello. How are you? How are the kids?" Then the real conversation began. Though I knew how different I felt inside, I was surprised by my own directness.

LUCAS: *You look good. I hear you're getting married soon.*

SHARON: *Thank you. Yes, in four days.*

LUCAS: *That's great. Maybe we can be friends now that you're getting married. We always said that if we were both with other people, maybe we could be friends.*

SHARON: *I don't think so, Lucas. We've done our dance.*

LUCAS: *I never really got it about our relationship. I guess I was never really there.*

SHARON: *That's right, actually. You weren't.*

LUCAS: *So I guess we'll just randomly run into each other?*

SHARON: *Yes. Take care, Lucas. Good-bye.*

LUCAS: *Good-bye.*

I had come full circle. Someone who once held so much power for me had become an ordinary person, a man I almost didn't recognize. It was easy now to talk to him without getting hooked and then say good-bye. The discoveries that began as a desperate strategy on that Fourth of July had become part of my being. I was free—free from the pain of old patterns, free to begin the new life that was just four days away.

We've seen that for many couples the move to the story-below-the-story by way of the First Argument Technique unlocked their buried tenderness for one another and permitted them to make a new beginning within the relationship. That wasn't the case for me and Lucas, but the process brought tremendous healing for me nonetheless. Where was the little girl called *Ug* who had been paralyzed by the phrases *What's the big deal?* and *Suit yourself?* Moving through my first argument with Lucas about a fence, I had found that little girl standing in disbelief before the mirror, and once and for all I had validated her power to see through her own eyes.

Having become more intimate with myself, I gradually became ready to enter into a very different kind of partnership. I now believe that, without the understanding that came to me through my struggles with Lucas, I could never have received the gift of love that came to me in the form of Michael—the man who is now my husband.

Michael and I met at a difficult time for both of us. His wife of many years had recently died, and I was still recovering from the turmoil of my relationship with Lucas. Though I was drawn to Michael, I actually found it hard at first to trust his kind and even temper. In our first argument I accused him of being afraid to face the "dark side of things." He countered that I was too hot-tempered and that I didn't understand the source of my distrust. We broke up and were apart for four years, until circumstances unexpectedly threw us together again. At that point we discovered that we had both matured, each having done a great deal of soul-searching. Michael had emerged from his grief, and I was finally ready to accept the love of a gentle and stable man. It wasn't long before we realized that we wanted to get married.

The wedding took place four months after my fiftieth birthday, on an exceptionally hot August day. It was a beautiful wedding performed by our dear friends and spiritual mentors, Jaichima and her brother, Vicente. They are Huichol Indians from the Sierra Madres in Mexico, and they have a retreat center in Sedona, Arizona, where Michael and I have often visited them. All along they have encouraged us to cultivate the compassion for oneself that makes it possible to truly love another. Thanks to them and to our years of inner work, Michael and I have a relationship based on mutual respect, honesty, and commitment and one that involves little conflict. It's not that we never disagree—we actually have very different personalities—but we have come to know ourselves so well that our conflicts evaporate quickly. We each own our own "stuff," and there is little blaming. Because we're not lugging a reservoir of resentment, specific issues can be easily resolved and then we return to our fundamental harmony.

Now you can see that the hope I have to offer comes out of my own suffering and healing. With confidence I tell the troubled couples who come to me: "If you're willing to drop into the root of your conflict, you really can't lose, because no matter what, you're going to end up knowing a great deal more about yourself. And then you've got an infinitely better chance of finding greater intimacy within your relationship. When you're not just reacting out of your own painful past, you're truly free to *see* and to *be with* the other."

The remarkable thing is that the conflict we so dread can itself provide the antidote. This is the same paradoxical model of healing that we use in the modern process of vaccination—as well as in ancient alchemical practices going back for centuries. Again and again, both in my own life and in my work with couples, I have seen living proof that when properly understood, "the poison is the remedy."

The work of the First Argument Technique is simple, direct, and effective. It offers a starting point to unravel the conflict in a relationship. Rather than jumping into the confusion, anger, and chaos presented by two people, this method turns the mirror inward, thus revealing each individual's history and role in the conflict. When the conflict ceases being about the other person, we each become empowered to take responsibility for our own life and to maintain awareness of how we affect others. This in turn creates the space within the relationship to address specific, current issues, rather than endlessly recycling the same old material.

I also see a heartening trend today where divorce seems to be a couple's first option less frequently than it was ten years ago. Because many people don't have the money to spend on a costly divorce, they are more open to working things out with their partners, and more invested in exploring and trying to resolve their issues, rather than rushing to dissolve their union. Perhaps this is also because they feel so acutely the insecurity of the world around them and long to have that "safe harbor" in the storm. Perhaps it is because so many of them know the pain of their parents' divorce, and they don't want to go through it themselves or inflict it on their children. In any case, it has seemed to me that more couples than ever before are sincerely searching for ways to make sense of their confusion and find release from conflict. This has strengthened my resolve to share my insights with those whom I may never have the chance to work with in person and to give them new tools for understanding.

As we saw earlier, the rewards that come from this new understanding can ripple outward, beyond one's innermost circle, to include other family members, friends, and coworkers. In fact the rewards can spread to the widest possible circle: this very earth on which we live, so enflamed by human conflict. Think of the many struggles whose roots go back for centuries: between Catholics and Protestants in Ireland, between Jews and Palestinians, between Muslims and Hindus. They all seem to spring from an ancient grievance, recycled over and over again. Just imagine how powerful it would be if long-term enemies were able to drop below the endlessly repeated grievances to the story-below-the-story, to the sorrow that lies at the root of all conflict. Sound impossible? It has happened.

Consider this extraordinary example. In the Truth Tribunals that took place in South Africa, the victims of apartheid and its perpetrators sat in the courthouse hearing one another's stories. It is hard to imagine a more polarized context, yet observers reported that gradually an awareness of mutual anguish prevailed, an awareness that both victims and victimizers had been caught in the grip of a horrifically dehumanizing system. Such awareness cannot erase years of brutal history—but without it, healing cannot even begin. Awareness creates the site of healing and clearing, and we begin by creating this clearing in our own lives. By nipping conflict in the bud with our partners, our families, our friends, our coworkers, and within our communities, we offer a desperately needed model of human behavior. In the end the clearing we make within ourselves, the freedom we find within our own inner conflict, the ability to turn poison into a remedy, is the greatest gift we have to share with others and ourselves.

To facilitate the healing process when our wallets are slim and time is unyielding, I have created the following workbook that will enable couples to break their argument cycle without stepping into a therapist's office. This workbook will become an easy, yet highly effective tool/guide to determine your core issues and create a plan for healing your relationship, as well as a reference manual to use when issues arise in your relationship. This doesn't mean that I don't recommend therapy for couples when their marriages are on the brink of divorce or separation. But it is the next best thing to having professional therapy, and it will enable you to start now to break the repetitive argument cycles that are causing you pain and misery.

In the following workbook, *The Therapy Room,* you will have the opportunity to utilize the three-step First Argument Technique for your own unique situation by answering the same questions that I would ask you if you were seeing me face-to-face, with enough space to record your answers. This is where you'll ultimately discover your core issues or story-below-the-story. Once your core issues are discovered through your first argument, you will experience how these core issues never change throughout your relationship . . . no matter how many years you've been married . . . no matter how many kids you have. . . no matter what the circumstance . . . and no matter what the argument. You will learn how to use your story-below-the-story effectively in your relationships. By the end of the workbook, you will be able to immediately apply your new, very powerful tools and techniques to stop your destructive argument cycle forever.

* * *

Though I didn't know it fully at the time, for me that Fourth of July was indeed a day of independence. In a desperate, fumbling way I found a key that released me from years of painful repetition, opening me up to true love and helping me clarify my work in the world. And now, in the pages of this book, I pass this key on to all those who wish to unlock the code of their own recurrent conflict and discover the intimacy that lies below.

THE THERAPY ROOM

I have appropriately entitled this workbook *The Therapy Room* and have constructed it with great thought, detail, and precision so that it simulates, as close as possible, an actual in-person therapy session with you and me in my office. You will be led in, through, and out of the session with a carefully designed questionnaire created to evoke thought and introspection that enable us to gather as much information as possible to reveal to you your core issue or story-below-the-story. Once you identify your core issue, you will find a detailed description of what it really means so that you can begin to understand its role in your life and the web it's woven into all the fights you've had in your relationship. There will also be comprehensive, real-life case studies that relate to each particular core issue, providing a great tool for seeing how this process worked in the lives of my clients and enabling you to get a true picture of the healing power of the First Argument Technique. After you complete this step, I will guide you through the tools and exercises necessary to utilize now and in all subsequent fights that hook you so that you can begin the healing process for both you and your relationship.

Any work that promotes healing on a deeper level, such as what this process will accomplish, is intense. It will be an eye-opening experience that will finally allow you to understand and make sense of why things were the way there were, or are the way they are, and why your arguments never got or get resolved. You'll learn how to break the argument cycle, all without personally stepping into a professional therapy office.

Specifically, *The Therapy Room* is divided into four phases:

Phase 1: A Refresher Course—The First Argument Technique

Before you can apply the three-step process, I will provide a quick refresher course on the First Argument Technique. By getting into the depths of this superior method of conflict resolution, you'll have the clearest understanding of how this technique works as you begin to apply this process in Phase 2.

Phase 2: Session in Progress—The Questionnaire

The Questionnaire is expertly designed with thought-provoking questions to help you peel away the root of the first argument to reveal your personal history that makes you react so strongly in the fights with your partner. As you know, this is also called your core issue or story-below-the-story. I have provided two identical questionnaires so that you and your partner can each complete one separately. Remember, however, that this is your own personal journey, and even though we supply two questionnaires for both you and your partner, this is an individual process for both of you.

You may be wondering if it's possible to go forward with this workbook without a participating partner. Yes, you can. The ideal scenario is one in which you and your partner participate in this work together. By doing so, change would simply happen quicker. But don't despair or give up if your partner is unwilling to engage in this process. It is possible to do this work alone and reap the rewards of this very important voyage into self-discovery. Be forewarned, however, that there are no guarantees as to the outcome, and this effort will most likely cause your relationship to shift, both in negative and positive ways. The positive aspects are (1) this is your own journey into empowerment and healing and (2) the work is ultimately about you and altering the patterns that don't work for you. It only takes one person to shift the dynamics of the relationship, and the relationship will definitely change due to your efforts. The negative aspects are (1) you might have less patience with your partner; (2) your partner might act out to get you "back to normal"; and/ or (3) he or she could feel threatened by your transformations and undermine you both obviously and subtly. You may feel like the two of you are drifting apart. If this happens, it will take courage on your part to stay focused and continue your work.

Also, you may be afraid that by doing this work alone, your relationship will automatically end, or you may be so hopeful that it will automatically get better. I'm here to say that neither will happen right away. This is a work in progress that simply takes time. I've seen relationships work in all different time frames and in very diverse ways: together, alone, or apart. I've seen every outcome possible. The bottom line? If your partner doesn't participate, do this for you. You can't lose. This workbook is the catalyst for change.

When you complete the Questionnaire and your core issue is revealed, you'll then be guided to Phase 3.

Phase 3: The Reference Manual—Core Issue Descriptions and Case Study Comparisons

Based on the hundreds of couples I've counseled over the years, I've concluded that there are at least six distinct core issues. In this phase I will provide a thorough explanation of all six, as well as real-life case studies that will apply to each core issue. Then, with the core issue revealed to you in Phase 2, you'll be able to analyze what your core issue means. This is where things become clear and clarity and empathy happen.

Phase 4: The Tool Belt—Tools and Exercises for Healing
Finally, you'll enter Phase 4, where you'll learn the tools and exercises necessary for healing yourself and your relationship. These tools and exercises were specifically developed for each core issue and should be put to immediate use in your relationship and particularly when you find yourself hooked in your next argument. This is where the healing finally begins.

After the successful completion of all four phases, you'll be ready to leave *The Therapy Room* and put what you've learned into action.

Phase 1
A Refresher Course—The First Argument Technique

The First Argument Technique uses the peel, reveal, heal method of problem solving as a means to understanding the root dynamics of your relationship. It's a proven three-step process that can resolve years of conflict into understanding, resolution, and love. It uses your first argument or major disappointment as the road map that reveals the course to take for a healthy relationship. The value within this important conflict is that it embodies each partner's core issue that can be used to build harmony in the relationship, rather than perpetuate pain, resentment, and unhappiness. You will see that your first argument is simply the most important fight you will ever have.

Below is a refresher course that will take you through the three steps of this amazing process. It is a very condensed version of the First Argument Technique you read about in Chapter 3. If you need to refresh your memory with a more comprehensive explanation of any or all of the three steps outlined below, turn back to Chapter 3.

Step One: Peel
Locating the Hook and Deciphering Your First Argument

The first step starts with locating the hook in your current argument. Remember: A hook is another person's behavior that provokes an intense and disproportionate reaction in us that connects to a deep childhood wound—the hook can be verbal ("What's the big deal?" or "Suit yourself."), nonverbal (a look, a gesture, an emotional withdrawal), or situational (as when she wants to dance but he doesn't, or he wants a clean house but she's messy). Continue by returning to the scene of your very first argument or your first major disappointment as a couple to determine its connection to the current conflict. This is done by peeling away the content of the first argument by asking yourself, "What's the recurrent pattern here?"—the place where you got hooked then and where you're still getting hooked today.

It might help to think of the hook as the first "snag" between the two of you. Did that same snag just occur in your recent argument? Think about the similarity of now and then in the words that were spoken, gestures that were made, intense feelings or actions that caused and still cause you to react. Think about what makes this behavior so upsetting. What nerve does it touch? This is the hook that causes the pattern of arguing to repeat itself, making it impossible to resolve until you move onto Step Two.

Step Two: Reveal
Uncovering Your Core Issue or Story-below-the-Story

From this core dynamic, drop down to reveal the story-below-the-story. This is done so that you can understand how your childhood experiences impact your relationship and unresolved arguments. Write down a few things that stick in your mind about your childhood where you had a similar reaction or feeling to the one you're having in the present and that you had in your first argument. Ask yourself, "What's really going on?" Does any particular person come to mind that caused you the same feelings? Remember that you're looking for either a painful incident and/or a repeated pattern from childhood. In my case, as a little girl called *Ug*, the repeated pattern of not trusting myself developed in childhood and became the major hook in all of my arguments as an adult. As they try to reveal the story-below-the-story, I tell my clients, "Just keep patiently asking yourself, 'Have I ever felt this way before? When? What was going on at the time?'" Some people find it helpful to ask this question before going to sleep and as soon as possible upon awakening.

After writing about your childhood and answering these questions, you'll have a clearer understanding of yourself and your issues. You can then see that your first argument was the beginning of a cycle of continuous arguments.

Step Three: Heal
New Patterns of Verbal Response: Getting beyond Defensiveness
Once you've revealed the story-below-the-story, continue to stay with it awhile. Allow other memories to gather around it, and take some time to absorb its implications before immediately spilling it out to your partner.

After several days, when you've allowed the story to settle inside you and you feel truly ready to share it, remember to do so without blame. Avoid saying, "You're doing the same thing to me that my brother always did!" Instead explain, "Now I understand why I get so upset when you say, 'You're too sensitive.'" Remember that each partner's story-below-the-story must be handled with care. By definition it involves the revelation of a great personal vulnerability, and it should never be used to humiliate. I myself have come to see it as a kind of sacred revelation, worthy of the highest respect.

Now with your story-below-the-story or core issue revealed (the real reason you're fighting), it's time to take the next big step and create some new patterns of interaction. It's now that you can begin to heal the relationship with the tools outlined in Phase 4: The Tool Belt—Tools and Exercises for Healing.

Phase 2
Session in Progress—The Questionnaire

You can't break the argument cycle if you're trying to resolve the wrong issue. The right issue is found through the discovery of your core issue or story-below-the-story.

Answer the following questions to peel and reveal your own core issue.

BEFORE BEGINNING THE QUESTIONNAIRE, PLEASE NOTE: *If you suspect that you and/or your partner has a personality disorder (for a description of personality disorders, please visit www.appi.org); EXTREME reactions of anxiety, depression, entitlement, passive-aggressive behavior (see red flags in Chapter 4), and other extreme reactions; bipolar disorder; drug or alcohol abuse; or physical abuse, these severe disorders must be treated in person by a professional therapist and are beyond the scope of this workbook and the First Argument Technique, and thus do not apply to the core issue work contained herein.*

YOUR QUESTIONNAIRE

1. What was your first argument or major disappointment?

(What happened immediately before the fight? Where were you? What did you say? What did your partner say?)

_____

_____

_____

_____

_____

_____

_____

_____

_____

_____

_____

_____

2. What got you hooked?

(What words or phrase did you or your partner say that you had a strong reaction to? For example, "You always need to be right." "You never listen to me." "You make me crazy." "You're never available." "You're too sensitive." What look did he or she give you?)

_____

_____

_____

_____

_____

_____

_____

_____

_____

_____

3. How did you *FEEL* when you got hooked? Were you:

❑ Confused
❑ Distrustful
❑ Doubting
❑ Fearful (scared)
❑ Hurt
❑ Jealous
❑ Raged
❑ Sad
❑ Spacey (did you disconnect?)
❑ Did you feel sick (lightheaded, dizzy, nauseous)?
❑ Worthless
❑ Clingy
❑ Numb

Anger was most likely your first reaction, which is common. But *after* that first reaction of anger (if at all), what was the *next* feeling you experienced? If you don't remember, then what was the predominant feeling you experienced in your most recent and serious argument? Please choose only one of the above feelings that really overrides all the others.

I felt

_____

_____

_____

4. How did you *REACT*? Did you:

☐ Accuse
☐ Cry
☐ Defend
☐ Deny
☐ Explain
☐ Ignore
☐ Judge or criticize
☐ Minimize
☐ Scream/Yell
☐ Run away
☐ Placate (try to smooth it over)
☐ Get abusive (verbally or physically), revengeful?

You might have had several, but what was your *first* reaction before you had time to think? If you don't remember, what was the reaction to your most recent and serious argument? Please choose one of the above reactions that overrides all the others.

I reacted by

_____

_____

_____

_____

_____

_____

_____

_____

_____

5. Regarding question 3 above, what was the earliest memory you had of this same feeling? Revisit your childhood for any clues about your family, siblings, parents, relatives, friends, teachers . . . anybody. For example, I would write my memory as follows:

I remember my sister getting mad at me for taking too much time in the bathroom. This made me <u>feel</u> bad about myself and that there was something wrong with me, so I began to <u>doubt</u> my own feelings and truth. As a kid I felt this way because she was older, she was very sure of herself, and I held her opinion in high regard. So I <u>reacted</u> by <u>placating</u> her, i.e., hurrying up in the bathroom so she wouldn't get mad at me.

What is your memory?
I remember

_____

_____

_____

_____

_____

_____

_____

_____

_____

_____

_____

_____

_____

_____

This made me feel
(Choose a feeling from question 3 above.)

_____

_____

_____

_____

I reacted by
(Choose a reaction from question 4 above.)

_____

_____

_____

_____

6. Did the argument get resolved? If it didn't, how did you finally end the argument? Did you let go of it? What did you tell yourself? Did you rationalize/ compartmentalize ("That argument didn't mean anything because she/he was tired.")? Did you catastrophize the argument ("We'll never be the same again . . . our relationship is over . . . he doesn't love me.")? Did you feel revengeful ("She/He hurt me, so I'm going to hurt her/him")?

_____

_____

_____

_____

_____

_____

_____

_____

7. What was the impact of the argument? Did you hold onto it? Did you let it go? Did you think about it all the time and worry?

_____

_____

_____

_____

_____

_____

_____

_____

_____

_____

8. When was your most recent, serious argument? What was it about?

_____

_____

_____

_____

_____

_____

_____

_____

_____

_____

This made me feel
(Choose a feeling from question 3 above.)

_____

_____

_____

_____

I reacted by
(Choose a reaction from question 4 above.)

_____

_____

_____

_____

9. Based on your answers above, what are the recurring feelings and reactions that you've had starting with your first argument (questions 3 and 4), which led to your childhood wound (question 5), and then led to your most recent, serious argument (question 8)?

First Argument Feeling (question 3):

_____

_____

_____

_____

First Argument Reaction (question 4):

_____

_____

_____

_____

Childhood Feeling (question 5):

_____

_____

_____

_____

Childhood Reaction (question 5):

_____

_____

_____

_____

Most Recent, Serious Argument Feeling (question 8):

_____

_____

_____

_____

Most Recent, Serious Argument Reaction (question 8):

_____

_____

_____

10. Which one of the following words (core issues) best describes the pattern you've just discovered in question 9? Choose at least one, but no more than two.

❏ Abandonment/Lack of Trust (hurt, fearful, sad, clingy, needs reassurance)
❏ Control (jealous, perfection, entitlement, revengeful)
❏ Detachment (self-doubt, confusion, spacey, numb)
❏ Fear of Commitment (runs away, denies, ignores)
❏ Rage (extreme impatience, critical, judgmental, revengeful)
❏ Victim (cries, fearful, feels sick, self-doubt, worthless)

Record your core issue(s) below. Write your answer(s) BIG and BOLD so you'll NEVER FORGET your core issue(s)!

Core Issue 1:

_____

_____

Core Issue 2 (optional):

_____

_____

CONGRATULATIONS! Now that you have revealed your core issue(s), you never have to figure them out again! Next, for a more thorough description of your core issue(s), please turn to Phase 3: The Reference Manual— Core Issue Descriptions and Case Study Comparisons. Here you will read about your core issue, where it came from, why it manifested, and how it forms your arguments and impacts your life.

YOUR PARTNER'S QUESTIONNAIRE

Answer the following questions to peel and reveal your own core issue:

BEFORE BEGINNING THE QUESTIONNAIRE, PLEASE NOTE: If you suspect that you and/or your partner has a personality disorder (for a description of personality disorders, please visit www.appi.org); EXTREME reactions of anxiety, depression, entitlement, passive-aggressive behavior (please see red flags in Chapter 4), and other extreme reactions; bipolar disorder; drug or alcohol abuse; or physical abuse, these severe disorders must be treated in person by a professional therapist and are beyond the scope of this workbook and the First Argument Technique, and thus do not apply to the core issue work contained herein.

---

1. What was your first argument or major disappointment?
(What happened immediately before the fight? Where were you? What did you say? What did your partner say?)

_____

_____

_____

_____

_____

_____

_____

2. What got you hooked?
(What words or phrase did you or your partner say that you had a strong reaction to? For example, "You always

need to be right." "You never listen to me." "You make me crazy." "You're never available." "You're too sensitive." What look did he or she give you?)

_____

_____

_____

_____

_____

_____

_____

_____

3. How did you *FEEL* when you got hooked? Were you:

❑ Confused
❑ Distrustful
❑ Doubting
❑ Fearful (scared)
❑ Hurt
❑ Jealous
❑ Raged
❑ Sad
❑ Spacey (did you disconnect?)
❑ Did you feel sick (light headed, dizzy, nauseous)?
❑ Worthless
❑ Clingy
❑ Numb

Anger was most likely your first reaction, which is common. But *after* that first reaction of anger (if at all), then what was the *next* feeling you experienced? If you don't remember, what was the predominant feeling you experienced in your most recent and serious argument? Please choose only one of the above feelings that really overrides all the others.

I felt

_____

_____

_____

4. How did you _REACT_? Did you:

- ❏ Accuse
- ❏ Cry
- ❏ Defend
- ❏ Deny
- ❏ Explain
- ❏ Ignore
- ❏ Judge or criticize
- ❏ Minimize
- ❏ Scream/Yell
- ❏ Run away
- ❏ Placate (try to smooth it over)
- ❏ Get abusive (verbally or physically), revengeful?

You might have had several, but what was your _first_ reaction before you had time to think? If you don't remember, what was the reaction to your most recent and serious argument? Please choose one of the above reactions that overrides all the others.

I reacted by

_____

_____

_____

_____

_____

_____

_____

_____

_____

5. Regarding question 3 above, what was the earliest memory you had of this same feeling? Revisit your childhood for any clues about your family, siblings, parents, relatives, friends, teachers . . . anybody. For example, I would write my memory as follows:

I remember my sister getting mad at me for taking too much time in the bathroom. This made me <u>feel</u> bad about myself and that there was something wrong with me, so I began to <u>doubt</u> my own feelings and truth. As a kid I felt this way because she was older, she was very sure of herself, and I held her opinion in high regard. So I <u>reacted</u> by <u>placating</u> her, i.e., hurrying up in the bathroom so she wouldn't get mad at me.

What is your memory?
I remember

_____

_____

_____

_____

_____

_____

_____

This made me feel
(Choose a feeling from question 3 above.)

_____

_____

_____

_____

I reacted by
(Choose a reaction from question 4 above.)

_____

_____

_____

_____

6. Did the argument get resolved? If it didn't, how did you finally end the argument? Did you let go of it? What did you tell yourself? Did you rationalize/ compartmentalize ("That argument didn't mean anything because she/he was tired.")? Did you catastrophize the argument ("We'll never be the same again . . . our relationship is over . . . she/he doesn't love me.")? Did you feel revengeful ("She/He hurt me, so I'm going to hurt her/him.")?

_____

_____

_____

_____

_____

_____

_____

_____

7. What was the impact of the argument? Did you hold onto it? Did you let it go? Did you think about it all the time and worry?

_____

_____

_____

_____

_____

_____

_____

_____

_____

8. When was your most recent serious argument? What was it about?

_____

_____

_____

_____

_____

_____

_____

_____

_____

This made me feel
(Choose a feeling from question 3 above.)

_____

_____

_____

_____

I reacted by
(Choose a reaction from question 4 above.)

_____

_____

_____

_____

9. Based on your answers above, what are the recurring feelings and reactions that you've had starting with your first argument (questions 3 and 4), which led to your childhood wound (question 5), and then led to your most recent, serious argument (question 8)?

First Argument Feeling (question 3):

_____

_____

_____

_____

First Argument Reaction (question 4):

_____

_____

_____

_____

Childhood Feeling (question 5):

_____

_____

_____

_____

Childhood Reaction (question 5):

_____

_____

_____

_____

Most Recent, Serious Argument Feeling (question 8):

_____

_____

_____

Most Recent, Serious Argument Reaction (question 8):

_____

_____

_____

10. Which one of the following words (core issues) best describes the pattern you've just discovered in question 9? Choose at least one, but no more than two.

❑ Abandonment/Lack of Trust (hurt, fearful, sad, clingy, needs reassurance)
❑ Control (jealous, perfection, entitlement, revengeful)
❑ Detachment (self-doubt, confusion, spacey, numb)
❑ Fear of Commitment (runs away, denies, ignores)
❑ Rage (extreme impatience, critical, judgmental, revengeful)
❑ Victim (cries, fearful, feels sick, self-doubt, worthless)

Record your core issue(s) below. Write your answer(s) BIG and BOLD so you'll NEVER FORGET your core issue(s)!

Core Issue 1:

_____

_____

Core Issue 2 (optional):

_____

_____

CONGRATULATIONS! Now that you have revealed your core issue(s), you never have to figure them out again! Next, for a more thorough description of your core issue(s), please turn to Phase 3: The Reference Manual— Core Issue Descriptions and Case Study Comparisons. Here you will read about your core issue, where it came from, why it manifested, and how it forms your arguments and impacts your life.

Phase 3
The Reference Manual

PART 1: CORE ISSUE DESCRIPTIONS

The beauty of finding your core issue or story-below-the-story is that it becomes the common denominator in all of your fights, no matter what the argument content.

In Phase 2, you revealed your unique core issue(s). We will now discuss the six core issues with correlating case histories. As a whole this information is invaluable for teaching you everything you need to know about your particular story-below-the-story. Please note that the core issue descriptions may not address all characteristics inherent to that particular core issue. I included only the most obvious and common descriptions for each.

Six Core Issues at a Glance

1. **ABANDONMENT/LACK OF TRUST** (hurt, fearful, sad, clingy, needs reassurance)
2. **CONTROL** (jealous, perfection, entitlement, revengeful)
3. **DETACHMENT** (self-doubt, confusion, spacey, numb)
4. **FEAR OF COMMITMENT** (runs away, denies, ignores)
5. **RAGE** (extreme impatience, critical, judgmental, revengeful)
6. **VICTIM** (cries, fearful, feels sick, self-doubt, worthless)

Six Core Issues in Detail

1. ABANDONMENT/LACK OF TRUST: One or both of your parents may have either been gone (due to death) or unavailable (due to personality disorders such as depression, anxiety, etc.; addiction; a preoccupation with another child, partner, or sibling). Your parents may not have taken good care of you, neglected your feelings, left you with a lot of babysitters, made you fend for yourself, and so on. Your physical and emotional well-being were neglected.

Where it came from: A childhood of neglect and being ignored.

Why it manifested: You may have felt alone, that no one was there for you, and that no one was devoted to you or really took care of you or your feelings.

How does abandonment/lack of trust affect your arguments? You may either get very clingy and insecure and could literally beg your partner not to leave you. Or, you might run away or leave the relationship before you get abandoned. You may get very distant and check out emotionally.

How abandonment impacts your life: You may experience a basic lack of trust and might be terrified of being alone.

2. CONTROL: As a child, you may have either grown up in total chaos and needed to control your environment to compensate for the turmoil, or you may have been very controlled by parents in the form of overprotection, rigid rules, too many rules, or their fear. As a child you may never have learned to trust yourself, because everything was about the external rules. Because it's hard to trust yourself, you may feel entitled ("You owe me." "I'm better than you."), expect perfection from others because you may think you're perfect, or could be compelled to control everyone else to feel in control of yourself.

Where it came from: A childhood of chaos or control where there were a lot of rigid rules to live by.

Why it manifested: Because you may never have felt in control of yourself, you may try to control others to feel secure. Somewhere inside of you your beliefs may be: If I can control you, then I can feel safe, and I'm okay."

How does control affect your arguments? You may feel you have to be right or you will be out of control. You may exhibit feelings of jealousy, paranoia, and rigidity in your beliefs. Often your feelings are black and white, right or wrong, good or bad. There seems to be no in between.

How control impacts your life: You may be intolerant of differences. You may not be very happy because you feel compelled to manipulate others to get them to say or do what you want them to say or do. You can have a hard time relaxing and being spontaneous. Others may distance themselves from you as a way of avoiding your controlling behavior.

3. DETACHMENT: You may not have been taught good and/or appropriate boundaries in childhood, because your parents did not have good boundaries. Maybe your parents fought in front of you (and other siblings), which could have been scary. Sometimes this conflict may have been extreme, leading to abuse or bullying. The poor boundary issues could have also been a result of unusually painful situations (a disabled or mentally ill family member) that created conflict/disagreements regularly with family members. Because of this extreme conflict, you may have tended to tune out or daydream—anything to escape from what was really going on. You could have created another, more pleasant world in your head to escape from the drama around you. You may have appeared and felt spaced out a lot of the time.

Where it came from: A childhood of being exposed to extreme conflict. You may have been very fearful, therefore you disengaged.

Why it manifested: There may have been many scary situations, so you disengaged or detached to calm and mentally remove yourself from the flood of your own uncomfortable feelings.

How does detachment affect your arguments? You may not respond to your partner when he or she is arguing with you. Sometimes your partner may feel the only way to get your attention is by threatening to leave. Because you may have the strong tendency to shut down and be unresponsive, your arguing partner is likely to get even more fueled.

How does being detached impact your life? You may have trouble listening to people, leading you to not respond and and/or to forget what has been said to you. You probably have the ability to tune everyone out if you need to and therefore may not be present in your life. You might appear to agree with everything on the surface, but underneath you may feel a whole different way, because you simply don't want to respond. As soon as you feel the familiar feelings of fear and/or distress that you experienced as a child, you may have a tendency to shut down and disappear.

4. FEAR OF COMMITMENT: You may have received inconsistent messages as a child, such as your mother confiding in you when she was upset with your dad. This is *inconsistent* with the fact that you're a child and should never be put in a position to take care of a parent. Pressure may have been put on you to be responsible for too much at too young of an age. Perhaps your mother was ill and you had to take care of the household, never having the opportunity to be a kid. Therefore, as you got older, you may have shied away from commitment, with your basic feeling of always needing an escape route and always keeping doors open as wide as possible. To be committed or to stay in one place for too long feels like death, danger, or being fearful of getting hurt. You may feel that once you make a commitment (to marriage, children, and so on), your partner will "want to own you."

Where it came from: A childhood of inconsistent messages and having too much responsibility at too young an age.

Why it manifested: You may have felt trapped and suffocated as a child, so when thinking of being in a committed relationship as an adult, you may feel scared and often paralyzed.

How does fear of commitment affect your arguments? You probably avoid confrontation at all costs, because you might have to commit to something. You might change the subject, ignore it, or minimize it—anything not to be pinned down. You may even experience panic attacks at the thought of committing. And if you feel very threatened and suffocated, you may threaten to leave the relationship.

How fear of commitment impacts your life: It may be very difficult, if not impossible, for you to have deep relationships. If you are married, you might be emotionally unavailable, with one foot always out the door. You most likely are more comfortable with superficial relationships, where your commitment level is small. Your rationalization is that you want to live in the moment. Because you never were taught about boundaries as a child, you may set your own boundaries by being unavailable. Unavailability is your self-created boundary, yet it keeps you from having intimacy in your relationships.

5. RAGE: Rage can come from a childhood where there was judgment and criticism. As a child you might have felt like you could do nothing right and felt a lot of anger and/or rage, but you didn't dare express your anger because your mom, dad, or siblings would just get even angrier. Anger/rage is a continuum. To have just used "anger" as a core issue is simply too general, because we all become angry at one time or another. However, rage doesn't necessarily mean you're ready to hurt someone. If you're having difficulty relating to the term "rage," then just substitute the word "anger" for "rage" as your core issue and continue on with the rage description.

Where it came from: A childhood of judgment and criticism.

Why it manifested: As a child you probably weren't able to express your anger, so you suppressed it until it eventually turned into rage.

How does rage affect your arguments? You might be accusing, extremely impatient, judgmental, and critical, just as was done to you as a child. You tend to yell and overreact at the smallest things, sometimes not even fully understanding the depth of rage you carry.

How rage impacts your life: It could alienate people, making it very difficult to have intimate relationships. Others might be fearful of you and feel unsafe to express themselves to you.

6. VICTIM: You probably grew up with insecure parents who were inflexible and expected you to fit into their picture of what a child should be. You most likely were unable to express or be yourself and were not allowed to have a voice or an opinion of your own. You may never have felt special, because you were treated like a nobody and therefore never had a chance to develop a good self-esteem. You may have received this subliminal message from your parent (or parents): "Your role is to be here for me; you don't have a self, a say, or a place in this world except what you can do for me."

Where it came from: Growing up in a childhood where you did not have the right circumstances or opportunites to develop a sense of self-worth.

Why it manifested: You most likely felt at the mercy of your parents' rigidity and dysfunction. You probably never felt like you had a voice or that you mattered.

How does being a victim affect your arguments? You might just "lie down and take it," so to speak. Because your sense of self is unclear, and it's difficult for you to have a voice or opinion, you may let people take advantage of you. You can be very evasive and unclear, hoping to end the argument as quickly as possible. You may be the typical "nice girl or guy," at your own expense.

How does being a victim impact your life? Because you may have no sense of self, the way you learned to have a voice was to be the victim, blaming everyone around you and not taking responsibility for yourself. You may often feel like "poor me" and expect people to take care of you.

PART 2: CASE STUDY COMPARISONS

Below are four real-life case studies. For confidentiality purposes, the names have been changed.

1. CASE HISTORY: LESLIE AND GRAHAM
<u>Core Issues</u>
Leslie: Abandonment/Lack of Trust
Graham: Detachment

Leslie and Graham are in their early forties. Leslie has a seventeen-year-old daughter from a prior marriage. Graham has no children. They have been together for five years, are living together, and are planning to marry. Leslie's prior marriage had ended very badly, and she didn't want to repeat the same mistakes in her new life with Graham. Thus before they got married, they wanted to work out some of their issues. Unlike many couples whom I see, their relationship was not at the breaking point. They wanted to learn the proper tools to deal with conflict before getting married to have a better chance at preventing their relationship from ever getting to that breaking point. Leslie and Graham were unusual to be coming in before big trouble had started in their relationship. This is an excellent example of how the three-step First Argument Technique can be used at any time in a relationship. I started our session at the same place with them that I do with any couple in crises. I asked them, "What was your first argument?"

STEP 1: PEEL
Look at the surface issue. What is the content of the argument?

For the first step Leslie and Graham had to revisit their first argument and write down what they remembered happening. If they couldn't remember their first argument, they could instead write down their first disappointment. When Leslie was moving into Graham's house, he did not do any real rearranging to make space for her. Their first argument involved Leslie getting her feelings hurt and Graham feeling mystified as to why.

Leslie might have written this:
Graham and I decided to move in together. I was very excited and arrived at his house only to see that he had not made an effort to clean up for me or to make any space for me. There were no closets or drawers emptied out, and I wondered if he really wanted me to move in.

Graham might have written this:
Our first argument involved Leslie getting upset with me because it seemed like I hadn't made room for her in my house when she was moving in. I saw it differently. I wanted her to feel like it was her house, too, so I thought we would rearrange it together. I didn't want her to feel like she was just moving into my house. It had nothing to do with my not wanting her to move in.

The second step for Leslie and Graham was to understand how their childhood experiences were impacting them and causing their first argument. Again, Leslie and Graham needed to write down some things using the three-step First Argument Technique:

THE PEELING CONTINUED:

**After Leslie peeled back the layer of their first argu-
ment, she might have written this:**

*On the surface the issue was that I was hurt and angry
because I felt that Graham was so inconsiderate and
hadn't made room for me in his house. When I tried to talk
to Graham about this, he got very defensive and angry
and said he wanted us to do it together so I wouldn't feel
like it was just his house. I wasn't sure if I believed him. I
just felt abandoned and scared.*

Graham might have written this:

*On the surface I felt hurt and angry that Leslie was upset
with me, because I really wanted to make room in my
house for her by working together as a team. I couldn't
convince her that it had nothing to do with not wanting
her there. In fact it was quite the opposite. I wanted her
to really know that my house was now her house, too.
The more I explained, the worse our argument got. I felt
upset that Leslie did not believe me. I felt hopeless and
helpless to try to convince her otherwise. I felt stuck and
had no idea what to do. So I did what I usually do when
there's a conflict: I detached myself emotionally and got
very quiet.*

STEP 2: REVEAL

**Under the surface, and from this first argument, the
core issues or story-below-the-story can be revealed.**

Leslie and Graham needed to write down a few things
that stuck in their minds about their childhood where
they had a similar reaction to the one they were having
in the present.

Leslie might have written this:

I came from a very close-knit family where I knew I was loved and admired by my parents. The problem was not that my parents didn't love me; it was that they were not very present due to my mom's bouts with depression and my dad's busy work and travel schedule. They were loving parents, but nonetheless I felt alone and ignored a lot of the time, often having to make my own decisions and fend for myself. I didn't learn a lot of coping mechanisms from my parents and just did the best I could. As I got older and, especially in my first marriage, I wanted to be loved and cared for so much, that I just trusted my ex-husband "blindly." When I found out that he had cheated on me, I was devastated. I realized that I had no skills to deal with such a huge betrayal. I could no longer trust my own instincts, because they had failed me so miserably. I had no idea who I was or what I wanted. Therefore, when I met Graham, I was very wary to get involved. I began looking at anything and everything he did as a potential breach of trust. I took everything personally and really didn't know how to take care of myself and put my needs first. I realized that I needed to learn to trust myself, rather than place my trust in everyone else.

Graham might have written this:

I came from a family where anger and violence were the name of the game. It wasn't just minor anger; it was physical fighting, threats, truly life-threatening stuff. I hated it and vowed I would never be that way with my own family. And I've stuck to that. I try to avoid conflict and hide my anger at all costs. Because of this, I tend to disappear at times. I do that because I don't want to react out of anger like my parents did, and it's a way for me to cool down, I guess. After I'm done escaping for a while, I then work very hard to be understanding and explain what's happening for me rather than losing my temper. Leslie often accuses me of being mad at her or not really loving her because I've disappeared. Since I grew up with such anger in my home, I have a different picture of real anger than Leslie does. If I'm upset and a bit cross, I don't consider that anger. Anger to me is equivalent to violence. The reason I didn't clean up my house for Leslie was that I wanted to make sure we did it together. In my home no one ever considered my feelings or my needs. Therefore I go to great lengths to consider other people's feelings. It hurts me that Leslie often wonders if I love her, and she doesn't believe me even when I say I do. This makes me feel like I did growing up in my family—unseen and unheard.

After writing about their childhoods, each person has a better understanding of themselves and their issues. They can then look at their first argument and see that it was the beginning of the cycle of continuing arguments.

STEP 3: HEAL
Once core childhood issues are revealed, with tools and exercises they can begin to heal their first argument to break the cycle of arguments.

Leslie had to stay very conscious of when she took things too personally and projected her hurt from her prior marriage onto Graham. She had to write down exactly what was going on before she immediately reacted to Graham. She also had to keep telling herself, that this is Graham, he loves her, and he is not Brent (her ex-husband). She then needed to stop second-guessing Graham and begin the process of believing Graham when he said he wasn't mad or wasn't trying to hurt her. She needed to stop assuming that Graham was untrustworthy or that their relationship was doomed anytime something went wrong where Graham disappeared or appeared angry. Leslie basically had to stop projecting her fears of abandonment onto Graham and begin talking about how she felt and what was scary for her. Once she understood that Graham's idea of anger was different from hers and that when he disappeared he was just regrouping, it made it easier for her to take responsibility for her own feelings and talk about them to Graham.

Graham had to remember that Leslie's ideas of anger and detachment were different from his. So when he was frustrated (to her this felt like anger), he had to understand that she was sensitive to that. Rather than defending himself that he wasn't angry (which was important to him since he had tried so hard to be different from his family) and that he wasn't abandoning her when he was detached, he just needed to hear that she was upset, and not disappear. All she needed at that moment from him was reassurance that he loved her and wasn't leaving her. As soon as he was able to stay present and reassure her, and as soon as she began to believe his reassuring words, their arguments were virtually nipped in the bud.

The next time Leslie and Graham have an argument, they each need to remember what is getting triggered and implement the tools and exercises to quickly resolve the conflict (see Phase 4: The Tool Box—Tools and Exercises for Healing). It's all up to them.

Leslie and Graham's next fight might go like this:
Leslie is upset because Graham hasn't finished all the projects around the house that he agreed to do. She, again, begins to wonder if he really wants her to live there. She now knows that her core issue of feeling scared and rejected (abandoned) has been triggered when she starts to compensate for these feelings by wondering how Graham is feeling and what it really means that he hasn't

finished the projects. By knowing this she can decide to approach Graham in a different way. Rather than accusing him of never finishing anything and, therefore, taking that to mean that he doesn't care about her, she could say, "It's really important to me that our house look nice and completed. I know that's important to you, too, so is there anything I can do to speed up the process? Maybe we need to review the time line and see what we could do differently."

Graham needs to go back to his core issue about feeling unseen and unheard and wanting to avoid conflict. Rather than defending himself with a lot of excuses about the unfinished projects or not addressing the conflict by disappearing, he could tell Leslie, honestly, that he feels overwhelmed and guilty that he hasn't finished everything in a timely manner. He does want to get it done and isn't sure he can do it all. Maybe he bit off more than he can chew.

At this point Graham and Leslie are talking honestly about their feelings, rather than blaming and shaming each other. They can go back to the drawing board and look at a realistic picture and time frame for finishing the projects. In the past this would have been at least a three-day argument, with Leslie feeling abandoned and Graham feeling misunderstood and then disappearing. Now they are merely having a discussion about household projects and how to best work on them together.

2. CASE HISTORY: JESSICA AND BRIAN
<u>Core Issues</u>
Jessica: Detachment
Brian: Rage

Jessica and Brian are in their early thirties and have a three-year-old son. When they came to see me, like many couples, they just couldn't stop fighting and were unable to let go of past hurts and resentments. They were specifically having problems with Jessica's family, who were about to visit, and were at a loss as to how to proceed to resolve some of the issues. They felt very stuck in repetitive patterns and were at a stalemate with each other.

STEP 1: PEEL
Look at the surface issue. What is the content of the argument?

For the first step Jessica and Brian had to revisit their first argument and write down what they remembered happening. If they couldn't remember their first argument, they could instead write down their first disappointment. Jessica and Brian's first argument happened before they got married, and it involved Jessica's parents' disapproval of Brian.

Jessica might have written this:

My parents didn't think Brian was the right choice for me and couldn't understand what I saw in him or why I was with him. Though I was clear that I didn't want to break up with Brian, I didn't really defend him to my parents which, understandably, made Brian hurt and angry. I understood his feelings, but honestly I didn't know how to defend him without hurting my parents. I hoped it would all work itself out, but it didn't. It got worse through the years, and we argued about it constantly.

Brian might have written this:

Our first argument involved Jessica's parents' disapproval of me and her inability to defend me to them. I always want to be a nice guy, so I didn't push the issue of not defending me with Jessica, and tried to suck it up and continue to understand and be tolerant and patient.

However, I did tell Jessica that I was hurt that she didn't stand up for me with her parents. Jessica seemed to understand, but she never really changed her behavior. As time went on the insults and criticisms of me from Jessica's family continued until I couldn't take it anymore and needed something to change! Jessica and I continued arguing about this, and it never felt resolved.

The second step for Jessica and Brian was to understand how their childhood experiences were impacting them and causing their first argument. Again Jessica and Brian needed to write some things down using the three-step First Argument Technique.

THE PEELING CONTINUED:
After Jessica peeled back the layer of their first argument, she might have written this:
On the surface the issue was that Brian was hurt and angry that I didn't defend him and stick up for him with my family. I felt stuck in the middle, not wanting to hurt my family or Brian, so I did nothing, because I really didn't know what to do!

Brian might have written this:
On the surface I felt hurt and angry that Jessica didn't defend me to her parents. I wondered if she really loved me. I wanted to be the nice guy and not make waves, but my anger and frustration kept building, and I just couldn't let it go. I felt Jessica had betrayed me.

STEP 2: REVEAL
Under the surface, and from this first argument, the core issues or story-below-the-story can be revealed.
Jessica and Brian needed to write down a few things that stuck in their minds about their childhood where they

had a similar reaction to the one they were having in the present.

Jessica might have written this:

I came from a very close-knit family and my youngest sister was physically disabled, so a lot of my parents' attention went to her, wanting her to have as normal a life as possible. I was the good child in the family, always there for everyone, never wanting them to be disappointed in me. My family life was very chaotic, and my parents had their hands full with my sister. I didn't want to cause them more stress, so I kept to myself a lot, creating a quieter, more peaceful world than the one around me. These quiet, detached times were the only real life I had, since I was always there for others. In many ways I was comfortable with this role. However, when I met Brian, I realized I wanted my own life separate from my family and liked that Brian was a bit rebellious and independent. I was clear from the beginning of our relationship that I wanted to be with him even if it meant moving away from my family and doing things that differed from what they expected. However, I still wanted to keep everyone happy, so I had a very difficult time standing up to my family in Brian's defense when they began criticizing him. I didn't want to have to choose between all the people I loved the most, so I hoped that it would all just work itself out. I also had the habit of tuning things out, which drove Brian crazy, since he never knew if I really heard him and, therefore he wondered if I even cared about him. I learned to tune out when there was so much chaos in my home. This was often the only way I could get peace and have my own life and thoughts.

Brian might have written this:

I came from a family in which I was both loved and

criticized. I felt my father was demanding and exacting, and I never felt I could please him. Though I know I'm intelligent, reading and writing did not come easy for me, as I have a learning disability. I was in special classes and often felt stupid and incompetent. My feelings of incompetence were sometimes reinforced by my dad's criticism, which then led my mom to overcompensate by doing a lot for me to make me feel better. So on the one hand, when Jessica didn't defend me to her parents, I understood, but I also wanted desperately to be loved and accepted. I was afraid that if I complained and rocked the boat, Jessica might leave me. Yet at the same time, my feelings of inadequacy and stupidity were triggered every time Jessica's parents demeaned me. I would feel very angry and sometimes filled with rage. Jessica kept saying, 'They don't mean to be insulting . . . it's just how they are.' After awhile, however, I felt so bad about myself that I couldn't take the insults anymore, so I told Jessica I couldn't be around her parents unless something changed. My anger was building up to the point that I was afraid I might explode in a destructive way. I just didn't know what else to do.

After writing about their childhoods, each person has a better understanding of themselves and their issues. They can then look at their first argument and see that it was the beginning of the cycle of continuing arguments.

STEP 3: HEAL
Once core childhood issues are revealed, with tools and exercises they can begin to heal their first argument to break the cycle of arguments.
Jessica had to stay very conscious of when she tuned out. She had to write down what was going on right before she tuned out so she could begin to identify the topics

that triggered her going away to get peace. At the same time, she needed to find a way to stay present in those moments and at least tell Brian she was tuning out or had been tuning out. That way he would know it wasn't something he had done . . . it was just Jessica getting triggered when she felt her environment becoming too chaotic.

Brian had to stay present in the moment and not bring up all the past incidents that seemed so huge and made him furious. He also needed to write down what triggered him and to keep telling himself, "That was then, this is now, and how do I feel now? Is anything different? If I didn't add all the past to the present moment, how would I feel about Jessica and myself?" He also needed to speak up immediately when he felt badly about something and not second-guess himself so his hurt wouldn't fester.

The next time Jessica and Brian have an argument, they each need to remember what is getting triggered and implement the tools and exercises to quickly resolve the conflict (see Phase 4: The Tool Box—Tools and Exercises for Healing). It's all up to them.

Jessica and Brian's next fight might go like this:

Jessica is upset because Brian was supposed to take care of their son but changed his plans at the last minute. Jessica is now in a bind because she has to work and has no child care. Rather than immediately getting angry with Brian, she takes a step back and thinks about the situation, remembering their core issues. She knows that this has something to do with Brian being angry because either she tuned out or he felt she wasn't acknowledging him. Because her core issue is to detach, Jessica has to see where she might have tuned out, rather than just remain angry at Brian for changing his plans. She has to go beyond the content of the plans changing and drop to her core issue (her story-below-the-story) and address the issue from that point. She might be mad that he's responding in his old way, so she needs to tell him that and not just say, "How come you're changing your plans at the last minute again when you know this is not good for me?" Instead she could say, "I'm not happy with the fact that I'm just finding this out at the last minute, but there must be something more to this because I know you wouldn't do this just to be mean to me. What's going on?"

Brian needs to go back to his core issue of rage when he feels unappreciated, criticized, and unseen and see if something triggered his old response of "punishing" Jessica. He could say to her, "I'm sorry I changed the plans, and I realize now that I was upset that you asked me to watch our son, and you had forgotten that I had plans with my brother. Instead of telling you that in the moment, I got angry and then changed my plans with you, rather than talk to you about my feelings. I know that wasn't right, and I should have been honest with you in the first place."

Once Jessica and Brian talk about the underlying issues of her tuning out and his getting angry and acting out, it will become clearer for both of them where this argument started. They can then talk about their real feelings and each apologize for his or her part in the fight. If they don't look below the surface of the fight, the angry feelings they both have could last for days.

3. CASE HISTORY: CHERYL AND DENNIS
<u>Core Issues</u>
Cheryl: Control
Dennis: Victim

Cheryl and Dennis are in their late forties and have a nineteen-year-old son and seventeen-year-old daughter. They have been separated for twelve years, yet have not gotten a divorce. Dennis was the first one who came to see me, because he couldn't understand why he wasn't filing for divorce from Cheryl. When they first separated, their children were young, so he "justified" not divorcing Cheryl at that time because he wanted his family to be as intact as possible. He felt his main concern was raising his children, and he didn't care that much about moving on with his own life. He had a good job and, because of his gregarious personality, had many friends and therefore never lacked social interaction. Even though he and Cheryl were separated, they frequently ate dinner together at his home with the kids. As their children grew older, Dennis began to feel the consequences of his inability to divorce Cheryl—he really didn't have a life of his own. He specifically wanted to see what was stopping him from taking the final step to file for a divorce. Cheryl eventually came into therapy with Dennis, and she agreed that they should divorce, but she reiterated that they hadn't because of their children and wanting to be "as much of a family as they could be" in spite of being separated. They were in agreement that they were ready to take the next step toward divorce, and yet were both mystified as to why they never did. As I always do, even in this situation of a separated couple, I asked them about their first argument, using the three-step First Argument Technique. The reason for this is that they still clearly had a relationship with each other and their children. Obviously something was stopping them from taking the final step in their separation, which was to file for divorce.

STEP 1: PEEL
Look at the surface issue. What is the content of the argument?
For the first step Cheryl and Dennis had to revisit their first argument and write down what they remembered

happening. If they couldn't remember their first argument, they could instead write down their first disappointment. Cheryl and Dennis's first argument happened before they got married. Cheryl had a very definite idea about their wedding and where and how they would live. She had a plan and was reluctant to deviate from it. Dennis had different ideas for their wedding: He wanted a small wedding, she wanted a huge one. Dennis, by nature, is flexible and understanding, so he "went along" with most of Cheryl's plans. However, when he had certain ideas about the guest list or the food and spoke up about them, she got very angry and accused him of not caring about her and not being there for her. He told her that wasn't the case, but she felt hurt and even "threatened" to call off the wedding. Dennis found himself backing down, apologizing, and again "going along" with Cheryl's plans. He did not want to upset her and rationalized that it wasn't that big of a deal to him. It was more important to Dennis to keep her happy, so he just gave in to all of her wishes. Cheryl felt that it was unfair of Dennis to suddenly balk at her plans, when he had given her the impression all along that "she could do what she wanted with the wedding and he would be fine." She felt betrayed by Dennis and unsupported. She began to wonder if he was telling her the truth when he said everything was okay. Her trust in him was questioned, but she loved him and didn't really want to call off the wedding.

Cheryl might have written this:
When Dennis and I first got together, he seemed like the perfect choice for me because he was so understanding, kind, and easygoing. My family loved him, and he was so friendly and outgoing—everyone adored Dennis! However, as time went on, I began to see that he would agree with me and seem okay with the agreements, but

then he would change his mind or not support me when I was upset. He was so loving and happy with everyone else, but I felt we lacked a certain connection at home. He was a great father, but I didn't feel we could talk about our problems successfully. He would just "give into me," but I never felt we resolved anything. As time went on I became very angry and hurt about his distance toward me. I was resentful that he was everyone's favorite person, yet I felt last on his list of priorities. I tried to get my point across to him by yelling and withdrawing, which of course only pushed him farther away. Nothing seemed to change our situation, and both of us were unhappy. I finally reached the point of feeling so hopeless about working things out that I asked to separate. Once we had separated, we actually got along better and fell into the habit of spending a lot of time together—as if we were still a couple. Neither of us knew how to get out of that pattern—especially since we have two children and both of us wanted to keep the family together as much as we possibly could.

Dennis might have written this:
I really wanted to make Cheryl happy. I am an easygoing kind of guy, so most of her plans and ideas were really fine with me. However, after I would agree to certain things, I realized I didn't really agree. I never knew how to talk to her about how I was feeling, so I would "suddenly" take issue with her, and she reacted very strongly with anger, threats, and tears. I didn't know what to do, would feel badly that I had hurt her, and would backtrack on my position by trying to please her. She never felt like I was "there for her," and I really didn't know what she meant by that statement or what I needed to do to make her happy. We grew farther and farther apart, and when she asked for a separation, I was very upset and really didn't

understand fully what had happened. I felt I was so in love with her and did everything for her, yet she wasn't happy. I have continued this pattern of trying to please her and feeling confused for the twelve years of our separation. She is at my house quite frequently, and I can't seem to find a way to break this pattern. It's as if we're still married, and I can't really have a life if I'm still, in essence, wedded to someone I'm not with! I didn't know how to relate to her in our marriage, and I still don't.

The second step for Cheryl and Dennis was to understand how their childhood experiences were impacting them and causing their first argument. Again Cheryl and Dennis needed to write some things down using the three-step First Argument Technique.

THE PEELING CONTINUED:
After Cheryl peeled back the layer of their first argument, she might have written this:
On the surface the issue was that Dennis did not understand my need for connection and conversation about our relationship. He seemed to want to please me but didn't really want to relate to me. I felt hurt and angry all the time, and I know I "attacked" Dennis constantly to try to get him to relate to me and make me feel special. He never "got" it, and I became more frustrated and hopeless as time went on. Finally after being unsuccessful at explaining my feelings and not being heard, I felt I had to leave the marriage. I was too upset too much of the time. This didn't seem good for our children, so I asked for a separation. It's weird that we have gotten along much better being separated, and that is why we end up spending so much time together, as if we're still "really" married. I don't understand it at all, because we're both clear that we don't want to be married, yet I am very

attached to him and consider him my best friend. None of it makes sense to me. We just can't seem to take the steps to file for divorce.

Dennis might have written this:
On the surface I felt hurt and angry that Cheryl didn't see or feel how much I loved her and did for her. Somehow the more I did, the worse it got for us. Whatever I was doing was not satisfying her, and I was very frustrated and angry at times. I just couldn't seem to find the right way to approach her, and it felt to me that she was always complaining, wanting more from me, and becoming angry at me most of the time. I hated conflict, so I would try my best to please her. I am still doing that, and I am still unable to "take a stand" with her. I avoid confrontations with her, because I feel they get us nowhere, and she just gets mad all over again. I have placated too much and, now that our kids are older, I feel I need to get on with my life. I need to finally end our relationship and get a divorce. I just can't seem to do it, though. I'm stuck.

STEP 2: REVEAL
Under the surface, and from this first argument, the core issues or story-below-the-story can be revealed.
Cheryl and Dennis needed to write down a few things that stuck in their minds about their childhood where they had a similar reaction to the one they were having in the present.

Cheryl might have written this:
I came from a family in which I was my dad's favorite and I could do no wrong. My mom was the one who tried to set boundaries with me, but I could always go to my dad and "get my way." I was very overprotected. Because my dad went out of his way to do things for me, I didn't learn

a lot about doing things for myself. Because I was able to get my way most of the time, I learned how to control situations for my own desired outcome. I guess I expected everyone to go along with my scenarios, so when Dennis would disagree with me or not go along with my plans, I got very hurt and angry. To me this was a sign that he didn't love me. Instead of understanding this fully, I just got angry and did everything I could to get my way, by controlling as many situations as I could. Even when I got my way, however, I still didn't feel like I was a priority for Dennis. He seemed to like my family more than me, and I got angry at him and my family about that. I didn't know how to get through to him!

Dennis might have written this:
I came from a family where my parents fought a lot. They never agreed on anything and criticized each other mercilessly. I had the kind of temperament that helped people feel better, so I was always "mediating" their fights and being a good son, hoping that would help them get along better. I am basically easygoing, so it was a natural role for me to play. However, I never really knew what my needs were or what I really wanted. I went along, and still do, with whatever I feel will make people happy. I always put myself second to everyone else, which is also what I did in my marriage. I get a lot of kudos for being the nice guy, but I can't really stand up for myself without feeling guilty. I have realized this isn't good for me. Because my parents were always in conflict, I try to avoid it at all costs. However, I am beginning to see that I do have feelings and do get upset. I just don't know how to set boundaries and speak about how I really feel. I feel I let too many people take advantage of me, including Cheryl and even my children. In our marriage, when Cheryl wanted more from me, I had no idea that she meant that on an emotional

level. I just knew how to "take care of people," not how to get close to them and express myself. The more she got angry in our marriage, the more I closed down and went into "provider" and "fix it" mode.

After writing about their childhoods, each person has a better understanding of themselves and their issues. They can then look at their first argument and see that it was the beginning of the cycle of continuing arguments.

STEP 3: HEAL
Once core childhood issues are revealed, with tools and exercises they can begin to heal their argument to break the cycle of arguments.

Cheryl had to take responsibility for her part in the reality that she and Dennis were separated and not divorced after twelve years. Though they lived apart, she still counted on him to help her in many different ways. She realized he was still her best friend, and she didn't want to lose that. Her whole family loved Dennis, and she enjoyed being with him with the whole family, including family vacations. She wanted him to be part of her family, but she didn't want them to be a couple. She realized she needed to "let go" of him and learn to stand on her own two feet. She recognized that she had always had a man to take care of her. First it was her dad, and now she had transferred that need onto Dennis. She knew this wasn't healthy for her and that she needed to respect Dennis's wishes to file for divorce. She had to stop trying to control the situation to get her needs met. Their children were now practically on their own, so she couldn't really use them as a rationalization for being at Dennis's house a lot. She began to see that she was not being responsible for her own life and needed to change her old pattern of looking to a man to take care of her. Therefore the next time Dennis talked to her about filing for divorce, she was determined to listen and talk to him, rather than argue and disagree with him. She began to explore new ideas for how to stay in Dennis's life without it preventing both of them from going their separate ways and having separate lives.

Dennis had to learn how to stand up to Cheryl and not be a victim. Even though they were separated, he still tried to please her and put his needs second to hers. He had to talk to her about his feelings and learn how to stand up to her even if she got angry with him. He realized, through the three-step First Argument Technique, that one of the reasons he was holding on to staying married to Cheryl was because her family had become like his own. They loved him and held him in high regard, coming to him for advice and respecting his opinions. That was hard to let go of since Dennis's family didn't treat him with the same respect. Dennis came to see that he could still have a relationship with Cheryl's family even if they were divorced. When Dennis finally set limits with Cheryl, he began to get his life back. She stopped coming over on a regular basis, they stopped talking every day, and they mutually agreed to file for divorce. They both still remained very involved with their children, but separate from each other. When Cheryl would now ask for certain things from him, Dennis was able to refuse if he didn't really want to do them. She was able to accept his refusal, understand his limits, and let go of trying to control his behavior.

The next time that Cheryl and Dennis have an argument, they each need to remember what is getting triggered and implement the tools and exercises to quickly resolve the conflict (see Phase 4: The Tool Box—Tools and Exercises for Healing). It's all up to them.

Cheryl and Dennis's next fight might go like this:
Dennis is upset that Cheryl wants him to join her family on their next vacation, telling him it won't be the same

without him. In the past he would have either ignored the fact that he didn't want to go on the vacation and say nothing to her, or he would have gotten angry at her, telling her she's got her own agenda and she knows it doesn't work for him. This time he calls Cheryl and tells her calmly and clearly that he doesn't want to go on vacation with her and her family, not because he doesn't care about them, but because it really isn't appropriate since they are separated. He tells her that family vacations are not an option for him anymore. He also clearly says that he is ready to move on with his life, and they need to figure out a more appropriate way of being in each other's lives. If they are separated, then their actions need to match that separation—not go on family vacations together, not see each other every day, and only talk when there's something specific to talk about.

For her part, Cheryl needs to listen to Dennis and not get defensive or manipulative. She wants an appropriate relationship with him and knows what he's saying makes sense. Throughout their relationship she has always wanted him to be honest and clear with her, and now he is. It is important for her to listen, and when she agrees with him, tell him, rather than arguing the point just to be right. She also has to respect his wishes that family vacations are not an option and stop trying to push his limits. She feels so comfortable with Dennis that it has been hard for her to be alone and really take the next step in her life.

As Dennis becomes clearer about his boundaries, and as Cheryl begins to really listen to Dennis, they are able to begin their real separation process. Cheryl only contacts Dennis when it is an important matter about the kids, or she just waits for Dennis to contact her. Dennis is able to stand up to Cheryl by talking about his feelings and is less and less fearful of her reaction. They are able to finally file for divorce after twelve years of separation and end their marriage.

Both Cheryl and Dennis can use their knowledge of their core issues to help them break a cycle that held them back from moving on with their lives.

4. CASE HISTORY: JOY AND RUSSELL

Core Issues:

Joy: Commitment

Russell: Abandonment/Lack of Trust

Russell had been coming to therapy without Joy. Joy is thirty-five and Russell is forty-eight. They are not married, but they have been together for fourteen years and have no children. Russell has always wanted to get married, but Joy has never been able to make that commitment to him. Periodically over the years she tells him: "I'm not sure if I really love you. I'm not sure if we have what it takes to make a life together," yet they continue to be together and, for all intents and purposes, are living as if they were married, sharing a home and finances. Russell came to therapy at a time when he found out that Joy was having an "emotional" affair. Though it was not a sexual affair, she was spending a lot of time with another man. Russell told Joy that this was unacceptable and that he would leave her if she didn't break off the affair. She did break it off and, once more, said she wasn't sure where her relationship with Russell was going. This prompted Russell to seek therapy. Joy did not. This is an excellent example of how the three-step First Argument Technique can be used at any time in a relationship, even if one person in the couple is not seeking help.

I started out my first session with Russell by asking him, "What was your first argument?" Even though he came in alone, I still needed a starting point to effectively help him. Through using his first argument with Joy, I immediately could determine both of their core issues and begin to help him. Remember: It takes only one person to change to shift the status quo of the relationship.

STEP 1: PEEL
Look at the surface issue. What is the content of the argument?

For the first step Russell had to revisit his first argument with Joy and write down what he remembered happening. If he couldn't remember their first argument, he could instead write down his first disappointment. When Russell met Joy everything was easy for them, until Joy needed to relocate for her work. Russell had a job that he loved but assumed that Joy would ask him to move with her, and he felt fine about relocating and getting another job. However, Joy was ambivalent about him coming with her. One day she'd invite him to move with her, and the next day she'd uninvite him. He felt hurt and abandoned and didn't know what to do. He loved Joy and didn't want to lose her. She never did officially invite him to move with her, and she never officially didn't invite him either. Therefore he decided on his own that he would move with her. Again she reacted with ambivalence.

Russell might have written this:
Joy was going to relocate to another city for her work. I assumed that she would be asking me to go with her, because I felt we were in love and committed to each other. However, as the days went on, I saw Joy's inability to commit to our relationship. Daily she vacillated between wanting me to go with her—not wanting to lose me—and not wanting me to go with her— being unsure if she really loved me. I was hurt and confused and could never get a definite answer out of her. As the time drew

closer for her to leave, I decided I needed to make my own decision. I knew I was deeply in love with Joy, so I decided to give up my current job and move with her, hoping that she really wanted me to go with her but just wasn't able to express that directly to me. I figured that if she didn't totally object, it was a sign that it was okay with her that we were moving together. I also figured and hoped that with time she would see that she really did love me and would eventually commit to me.

Because Joy was not in the therapy session, Russell and I were guessing as to what Joy would write down. In my experience with a person that has fear of commitment, I can only imagine what might have caused it, so we were really going on Joy's behavior: ambivalence, confusion, and not wanting to take full responsibility for Russell moving with her. If he made the decision, she could always put that back on him if things didn't work out.

THE PEELING CONTINUED:

After Russell peeled back the layer of their first argument, he might have written this:

On the surface the issue was that I was hurt and confused that Joy was suddenly so ambivalent about me moving with her. Up until this time, she seemed very into me and the relationship, and sometimes we even talked about a future together. Yet when the moment came to commit to the next level of our relationship, she backed away and seemed unsure of her feelings for me. When I tried to talk to Joy about this, she got very defensive and distant, saying she just wasn't sure if I was the one for her, yet she didn't want to lose me. She left the entire decision about moving with her up to me. I felt abandoned and scared, yet unable to stay behind, since I was so in love.

Again, Joy might be thinking that she cared for Russell but wasn't ready to totally be with him or totally be without him. As she said to him, "I'm just not sure if I can give you what you want, so you need to decide if you can live with that, because I can't promise you any more or be any more definitive right now."

Russell, of course, hoped this was temporary and that once he moved and they were together longer, her ambivalence would shift.

STEP 2: REVEAL
Under the surface, and from the first argument, the core issues or story-below-the-story can be revealed.
Russell needed to write down a few things that stuck in his mind about his childhood where he had a similar reaction to the one he was having with Joy.

Russell might have written this:
My family was very close, and I was especially close to my mother. When she died, I was devastated and felt empty and alone. I felt the same way when Joy told me she wasn't sure if she wanted me to move with her and wasn't sure if I was the one. I had an empty pit in my stomach, just like when my mom died. I almost felt that life had no meaning, and I wasn't sure what I was going to do with myself. With my mom and with Joy, to make myself feel better, I told myself the story that I would work hard and do everything right as my mom had taught me. I told myself that Joy would come around. By being with me more and more, she'd see that I was the one, and she would be so glad and relieved that I had moved with her. I never really dealt with the reality that Joy had commitment issues. I couldn't let myself believe that Joy didn't love me as I loved her. I clung onto her and actually probably projected some of my feelings for my mother onto

Joy and hoped she would take care of me as my mom had done—with total love and devotion.

Joy might have written this (information from Russell, since I did not work with Joy):
I came from a family where my mother was very over-protective and clingy. I felt like I had to take care of her, as my dad was absent because he worked a lot. I often felt trapped and unable to have my own thoughts and feelings. I felt my first job was to make sure my mother was okay, and then I could maybe think about myself. Every time I thought about Russell moving with me, I felt trapped, claustrophobic, and just wanted to run away. At the same time I really cared about him, and part of me did want him to move with me. I was so ambivalent; I couldn't give myself or Russell a straight answer. I was terrified of feeling trapped and under someone's control like I felt with my mother. When Russell decided to move with me, I figured we'd give it a try and see what happened. But part of me was very nervous about his decision, and I know I distanced myself from him. I felt badly because I did care for him, yet my fears of engulfment and commitment were huge!

After writing about his own childhood and discussing Joy's childhood, Russell had a better understanding of himself, and their issues. He could then look at their first argument and see that it was the beginning of the cycle of continuing arguments.

STEP 3: HEAL
Once core childhood issues are revealed, with tools and exercises, Russell can begin to heal their first argument and break the cycle of arguments.
Russell had to start setting boundaries with Joy. He had to

let her know his feelings and not always defer to her feelings. When she had the affair, he finally felt his own boundary kick in, realizing he had gone along with too many things with Joy, putting his own needs second to hers. He had to really see that she was not able to commit to him fully. He had to start telling himself the true story and not fantasize that someday she "would see the light." After fourteen years he realized he was the one who needed "to see the light" about who Joy really was and what she was and wasn't able to give him. Once he could tell himself the real story, he could decide if he wanted to stay with Joy, even with her inability to commit fully to him.

Russell did begin to set better boundaries with Joy. He spoke up more for himself with a newfound strength. He realized that it would be better to live without her than to continue denying his own needs. His fear of abandonment had been so strong since his mother's death that up until Joy had the affair, he was willing to put up with anything, sacrifice himself, and settle for crumbs just to be with Joy. He realized that he had to "get himself back" and take care of himself better by setting limits and realizing what he would and would not negotiate with Joy. As a result Joy has begun to listen to Russell more seriously and commit to him more, though it's a slow process. He told her that she could no longer tell him she wasn't sure if he was the one. If that were true, then she should just leave him. But she no longer says that. Russell feels much stronger within himself and is living his own life, not just as an appendage to Joy. Joy consults him more about decisions and respects him more.

The next time Russell and Joy have an argument, he needs to remember what is getting triggered and implement the tools and exercises to quickly resolve the conflict (see Phase 4: The Tool Box—Tools and Exercises for Healing). It's all up to him.

Russell and Joy's next fight might go like this:
Russell is upset because Joy will not even talk with him about getting married. He again begins to wonder if she really loves him and wants to continue their relationship, because she never wants to take things to the next level: marriage. Once his core issue of feeling abandoned and rejected are triggered, he starts to compensate for these feelings by appeasing Joy and convincing himself that he really doesn't care if they get married. After all, they are together, and isn't that all that matters? In this argument he decides to approach Joy in a different way. Rather than accuse her of not loving him and not being able to commit to him, he talks about what is important to him. "I want to be married, and I'm not going to minimize my feelings about that just because you might get mad at me or even leave me. I can't pretend anymore that I'm not bothered by the fact that you won't talk with me about this and hear my real feelings. I know you love me or you wouldn't be with me, so can we talk about what's going on so I have a better understanding of the situation? I don't want to pressure you, but I also don't want to act like this isn't important to me."

When Russell approaches Joy this way, she has more understanding and compassion for his feelings. She opens up about her fear of commitment and her fear that "bad things will happen to our relationship once we get married. I saw it with my parents' marriage. They weren't good to each other, and I don't want that to happen with us. I know this means a lot to you, so we can keep talking about this. I don't know if I'll ever be ready to marry you, but I am willing to keep talking about my fears and your desires."

At this point they are talking honestly about their feelings, rather than blaming and shaming each other. They can now talk about the "taboo" subject of marriage without either of them getting defensive. Russell still does not like the fact that Joy can't commit, but at least he is beginning to speak up for himself and let her know his feelings. Joy may not be ready for the next level of commitment, but at least she can talk honestly to Russell about her fears. In the past this would have been a standoff between the two of them, with Russell feeling abandoned and Joy feeling pressured and trapped. Now it is an honest discussion about their future together.

• • •

Now you're ready to enter Phase 4, where you'll learn the tools and exercises necessary to heal yourself and your relationship. These tools and exercises were specifically developed for each core issue and should be put to immediate use in your relationship, particularly when you find yourself hooked in your next argument. This is where the healing finally begins.

Phase 4
The Tool Belt—Tools and Exercises for Healing

Now that your core childhood issues have been revealed, you can begin to break the argument cycle and start the healing process with the following tools and exercises. And remember: It takes only one person to alter the dynamics of the relationship, so you can begin to use these tools on your own when your next argument occurs.

The beauty of therapy is that you are held accountable to your appointment time and therapy session. In this process, however, without a commitment to a therapist, it will be your goal to stay dedicated to this work on your own and for yourself, which is not an easy task to accomplish. When you find you're slipping from what you've learned, keep this book and workbook handy and in full view as a reminder that you need to stay focused on this process and continue your work. This should become a part of your daily life and is ultimately a life-long process.

Let's begin. Please note that the following exercises and tools apply to all six core issues. The Tool Belt is divided into four sections: (1) Preparation for the Argument; (2) Before the Argument Escalates; (3) During the Argument; and (4) After the Argument—Staying on Track.

1. PREPARATION FOR THE ARGUMENT
In order to prepare for your next argument, the three practices of *remembering, repeating,* and *reflecting* need to become a part of your daily habit. One of the biggest

obstacles couples face in changing their repetitive arguments is forgetting to use the tools they have learned. By studying and practicing these skills on a daily and consistent basis, you'll be able to successfully resolve your future arguments.

✓ Remembering

Always remember your core issues! Once you've figured out this valuable healing tool, it must be used and exercised in all future arguments for real resolution and understanding to take place. Due to the differences in the surface content of arguments, any particular fight could take you off guard and throw all your fight preparations out the window. You may not *think* that the conflict is hooking you, because it's not the same horrible fight you had last week, but the truth is that *it is hooking you.* So it's tricky. You need to pay attention and stay aware. When your reactions are disproportionate to the argument topic, that's your clue that you're dealing with your core issues. Further, just *knowing* what your core issues are will not necessarily *prevent* you from *reacting* each time you get triggered. Instead, you'll use your core issues as a means to: (1) end the confusion of your strong feelings of upset, hurt, or anger; (2) help you break the repetitive argument cycle; and (3) cut to the root of *any* conflict that you might have. We all get triggered, but now you have the information that can help you solve your relationship conflicts.

✓ Repeating

Repeat the following statements five times per day. (Each statement is followed by a brief explanation of its relation to your next argument. For further discussion see also "BEFORE THE ARGUMENT ESCALATES.")

"I don't have to immediately engage."
Before or during the argument, it's okay to tell your partner you're not ready to talk in that very moment. You don't want to say something you'll later regret. There's nothing wrong with waiting and thinking about your recent argument and talking about it at a later time.

"I don't have to express everything I'm feeling in the midst of a fight."
When you say everything that is on your mind, without being careful to filter out harmful accusations and righteousness, the fight will most likely escalate, leaving a deeper wedge between the two of you.

"I need to stay in present time."
Focus on what just happened in the argument without bringing in the past or the future.

"I can take a time-out."
If you or your partner has been triggered in your next argument, you can always take a step back and call a time-out. A time-out should be called if you can't seem to put any new patterns and responses into practice and/or you're so angry that you're saying things you know will only escalate the argument.

Why would repeating these four statements every day change your behavior in a fight? Repetition is a powerful way to change a long-standing pattern. By repeating these phrases daily, you actually give your brain a new message to replace the old messages that you continuously say, the ones that come out of your mouth without you even thinking about them. Think of it this way: You are so used to your old habits, because you have repeated them so many times for so many years. Now, as you repeat new phrases, ones designed to help you resolve your arguments, they will become your new habits. Therefore when your next fight occurs, you are more likely to say the new phrase and practice your new skills, rather than repeat the old ones that didn't work. Change doesn't happen quickly, so be patient and remember that it takes time to build new habits.

✓ Reflecting

Ask yourself the following questions in the midst of your next argument. The answers to these questions will begin the process of constructive fighting. Reflecting on these questions *daily,* before your next fight, will create a new belief pattern so that these thoughts become second nature to you when your next fight occurs. Keep in mind: "Practice makes permanent."

- What is happening *now?* Stay in present time. Remember: This is not your family of origin; you are no longer a child in your original family. Though your partner may trigger the same feelings you had with your family—which you discovered in your story-below-the-story—this is not that family, there are differences, and this is your partner, not your mother or father. You *can* change your behavior even if you've been triggered. Ask yourself, what is happening with the two of you *now, in the moment, in present time, in the current situation?* You may need to readjust your thinking and see how you feel just with the current situation.

- How do you feel about yourself and your partner now if you didn't bring up the history of the past?

- What if you gave your partner the benefit of the doubt?

- How might you respond if you didn't take this personally?

- How might you respond using what you now know about your own childhood triggers?

- What if you heard your partner and simply said, "I understand, I get it"?

- What if you didn't think of your partner as your enemy?

- Repeat the phrase, "The truth about . . ." *The truth about my husband is that he's a good man and is not out to get me.* "What would happen if . . . " *What would happen if I felt he wasn't out to get me, how would I react differently in this situation?*

By remembering, repeating, and reflecting, you create a new belief or thought pattern that, with consistent practice, will change your fighting pattern from destructive to constructive.

2. BEFORE THE ARGUMENT ESCALATES

When conflict arises, pay attention to it and acknowledge it, because it holds the key to your individual and relationship issues. You are now hooked or you wouldn't be having an argument. What you do at this point is crucial. Your fight could escalate or begin to diffuse. Here are tips to diffuse your argument before it spirals out of control:

✓ Stay present.

Discipline yourself to stay present in the moment of conflict and not bring up all the past incidents that seemed so huge and made you furious. What is triggering you? Start telling yourself, "That was then, this is now, and how do I feel *now?* Is anything different? If I didn't add all the past to the present moment, how would I feel about my partner and myself?" Staying present is easier to accomplish if you have been *reflecting* on this statement (and the accompanying questions in PREPARATION FOR THE ARGUMENT) in your daily practice.

✓ Resist the temptation to express your every feeling in that moment.

If you react without remembering your core issues (i.e., what the fight is really about), your tendency is to attack your partner, and the fight escalates. Get familiar with "argument clues" that alert you to repeating your old patterns that fuel the fight. These clues include harmful accusations, references to the past, criticizing, shaming, blaming, and needing to be right.

✓ Take a time-out.

It's necessary to step back and tell your partner you need a time-out if your emotions suddenly intensify and you and/or your partner are responding with familiar phrases that you know don't work, such as "I can't stand it when she . . ." or "Here we go again." or "You never . . ." or "You always . . ." During your time-out use your core issues to help you understand what you're *really* upset about so that when you do converse, you talk about what triggered you and not about the surface content that triggered you.

To take a time-out, remove yourself from the scene of the argument, take a deep breath, review the tools you've learned, and answer the following questions to understand where you got hooked or triggered:

- What exactly happened?
- What bothered me the most?
- What's really going on here?
- Have I felt this way before? When?

When you feel you're in present time, you've cooled off, and you're ready to talk, check in with your partner to see if he or she is now ready to converse. If yes, talk. If not, ask your partner to let you know when he or she is ready.

A time-out should be no longer than two hours. If the argument occurs late in the evening, it may be necessary to sleep on it. Just make sure you address the issues the next day, as promised. Set up a time to do this.

✓ Declare a truce.

If you can't take a time-out due to time constraints, declaring a truce is an effective way to postpone your discussion to a later time. Declaring a truce means you both agree to put the argument aside for the time being and come back to it later. You are not sweeping it under the rug, just postponing the discussion to a better time. For example, you start arguing, you've got an engagement to attend, and if you took a time-out you'd miss the event. By declaring a truce you agree to discuss the issue at a mutually agreeable time.

If the argument remains unresolved and continues to escalate, it's still not too late to break the argument cycle. In the next section we'll discuss what to do when you find yourselves in the middle of a fight.

3. DURING THE ARGUMENT

If your attempts to resolve the argument didn't work, or you didn't have a chance to use your tools at all, this is the absolute point where you must *do something differ-ent!* If you don't, nothing will change.

✓ Stop blaming, shaming, and needing to be absolutely right.
By eliminating these behaviors, you shift the pattern of destructive fighting. For a detailed explanation of these behaviors, see Chapter 1.

✓ Use I statements to communicate how you feel.
For example, "I know I should be saying this differently, but I can't right now. I'm just too angry." This statement conveys that you're taking responsibility for your own feelings, rather than blaming your partner for your anger. Another example is saying, "I feel sad because we argue all the time," rather than, "You're always out to hurt me."

✓ *Do something different.*
By simply saying to your partner, "We need to do something different," it immediately shifts the argument from the same destructive pattern to a break in the fight momentum. This allows each partner to take a step back, ask each other what he or she is really fighting about, and begin to implement the tools.

✓ *Remember what you have learned.*
Remember to utilize the tools you've learned throughout this Tool Belt. Get present, don't express every feeling and thought you have, and take a time-out if necessary.

I cannot emphasize enough the importance of being prepared, as outlined in PREPARATION FOR THE ARGUMENT. The amount of diligence, discipline, and dedication that you put into this process is directly proportionate to the success of breaking the argument cycle on your own, without therapy.

4. AFTER THE ARGUMENT—STAYING ON TRACK

When you and your partner are committed to this process, your goal when arguing is to be mindful of each other's core issue. By being mindful you are more likely to avoid triggering your partner's deep childhood wound (thereby making him or her more vulnerable) and having another disastrous argument. It is the responsibility of both of you to exercise the utmost sensitivity, regard, and great care when it comes to working with core issues. Now that you're using your Tool Belt consistently, here are some additional ways to stay on track with yourself and your partner:

✓ Write freely in a journal, where you can honestly write about your feelings and experiences.

✓ Tell your partner once a week how much you love and appreciate him or her.

✓ Take responsibility for your own feelings.

✓ Read books to learn more about personal growth and healthy relationships.

✓ Expect to feel unsettled and disoriented as you begin the process of change.

✓ Practice self-forgiveness daily.

✓ Of primary importance: Create support for yourself through good friends, family, a group—anyone who nurtures you—since you are doing a big thing and need to honor your vulnerability and courage.

Conclusion

The exercises and tools outlined in the Tool Belt are all you need for future conflict resolution. In order to successfully resolve arguments with your partner, you need to stay focused and committed to the process. In the long run it simply cannot work without a goal of commitment.

As you can see from your work with the First Argument Technique, it is an effective tool for understanding yourself and your partner at the deepest core level. Once these core issues are discovered through the first argument, they never change throughout the relationship . . . no matter how many months or years you have been together, no matter how many kids, no matter what the circumstance, and no matter what the argument. The content of the arguments may change throughout a marriage, but the core issues and tools used to resolve the arguments do not change.

If more couples used the First Argument Technique at the beginning of their relationship or before conflicts escalated into the danger zone, years of frustration and agony would be spared, marriages would be saved, and the divorce rate would plummet.

I wish you much success on your journey to self-discovery, conflict resolution, and ultimate healing of yourself and your relationship.

Acknowledgments

This book has been a long time coming and could not have been written without the help, guidance, and encouragement of many people. First of all, I thank my parents, Ellis and Zelda Rivkin, whose love and ability to let me think for myself and be myself are gifts beyond measure. From this freedom I have created this book and my life. I am grateful to my sister, Rosalyn, without whom I could not have become the person I am today. My children, Talia and Tashina Kilburn, have allowed me to love unconditionally, and I have learned so much from them. Watching them become the beautiful people that they are has brought me joy. I thank my husband, Michael, whose generous spirit and constant love go beyond words.

Without the help, dedication, and collaboration of both Noelle Oxenhandler and Mary (Deedee) Brandon, this book would not have come to fruition. I am grateful to Noelle for her knowledge, writing acumen, and friendship. I appreciate her unwavering belief in the concept of the first argument. This book would not exist without her consistency, competence, and concern.

I am grateful for Mary (Deedee) for her editing expertise and creative vision. Her persistent questions evoked a clear, concise read, and her sharp insight helped guide this book into a more expansive publication. She is invaluable to me professionally and as a dear friend.

To Jaichima and Vicente, whose love has enabled me to heal and to be me in all ways.

To my dear friends Joyce, Mindy, Suzi, Jennifer, Kathleen, Cherie, Joan, and Robbin, who have encouraged and supported me in the process of creating this book; they have never given up on its concept and eventual publication. And to Elizabeth, who though is no longer here physically, is ever-present.

To Karin Connelly, Kathleen Kraemer, and Jennifer Mann for their precise editing and helpful comments. To Julie Miknis for her detailed feedback about the workbook.

To my clients, whose stories are germane in the concept of the first argument and breaking the argument cycle. I respect and love each of you and am grateful for all that you have taught me. I am honored to have been a part of your healing process. I feel blessed that my job allows me to witness the deepest and truest parts of people.

About the Author

Sharon M. Rivkin, M.A., M.F.T., a licensed marriage and family therapist and conflict resolution expert, has been in private practice for over twenty-eight years in Santa Rosa, California. She has a Master of Arts in clinical psychology and specializes in individual, couples, and family therapy. Sharon has supervised MFT interns and, prior to opening her private practice, was director of the Learning Skills Program at Santa Rosa Junior College, which serves learning disabled and head-injured adults. There she created a highly acclaimed specialized counseling class for the parents of the students.

An experienced public speaker, Sharon has led workshops on the First Argument Technique, the role of language in healing, and women in mid-life. Sharon's work has been featured in several national magazines and Web sites, including *O: The Oprah Magazine* in the United States and South Africa, *Reader's Digest,* Yahoo. com, Dr.Laura.com, as well as on radio and TV.

Breaking the Argument Cycle: How to Stop Fighting Without Therapy is based on Sharon's extensive knowledge and expertise as an MFT and her own personal experience. Through her private therapy practice, she has helped countless couples resolve their conflicts, solve the mystery of why the same issues keep arising, and save their troubled relationships.

Sharon is married to Michael Howard and is the mother of two grown daughters, Talia and Tashina Kilburn. For more information visit www.sharonrivkin.com.